INVINCIBLE

BRENDAN RODGERS' HISTORIC
FIRST SEASON AT CELTIC

DAVID FRIEL

BACKPAGE

First published in Great Britain in 2017.
This edition published 2017 by
BACKPAGE

www.backpagepress.co.uk
@BackPagePress

ISBN: 9781909430273
eBook ISBN: 9781909430280

A catalogue record for this book is available on request
from the British Library.

Typeset by BackPage
Cover photograph by SNS

Printed and bound in Scotland by MBM Print SCS Ltd.

For Mum, Dad and Emma

CONTENTS

INVINCIBLE

Adjective: Too powerful to be defeated or overcome

Premiership

Hearts 1-2 Celtic
St Johnstone 2-4 Celtic
Celtic 4-1 Aberdeen
Celtic 5-1 Rangers
Inverness CT 2-2 Celtic
Celtic 6-1 Kilmarnock
Dundee 0-1 Celtic
Celtic 2-0 Motherwell
Ross County 0-4 Celtic
Aberdeen 0-1 Celtic
Celtic 3-0 Inverness CT
Kilmarnock 0-1 Celtic
Motherwell 3-4 Celtic
Partick Thistle 1-4 Celtic
Celtic 1-0 Hamilton
Celtic 2-1 Dundee
Celtic 1-0 Partick
Hamilton 0-3 Celtic
Celtic 2-0 Ross County

Rangers 1-2 Celtic
Celtic 1-0 St Johnstone
Celtic 4-0 Hearts
Celtic 1-0 Aberdeen
St Johnstone 2-5 Celtic
Celtic 2-0 Motherwell
Celtic 2-0 Hamilton
Inverness CT 0-4 Celtic
Celtic 1-1 Rangers
Dundee 1-2 Celtic
Hearts 0-5 Celtic
Celtic 1-1 Partick
Celtic 3-1 Kilmarnock
Ross County 2-2 Celtic
Rangers 1-5 Celtic
Celtic 4-1 St Johnstone
Aberdeen 1-3 Celtic
Partick 0-5 Celtic
Celtic 2-0 Hearts

League Cup

Celtic 5-0 Motherwell
Celtic 2-0 Alloa
Rangers 0-1 Celtic
Aberdeen 0-3 Celtic

Scottish Cup

Albion Rovers 0-3 Celtic
Celtic 6-0 Inverness CT
Celtic 4-1 St Mirren
Celtic 2-0 Rangers
Celtic 2-1 Aberdeen

LONDON CALLING

— Palma, May 11, 2016

THE sun is rising over Majorca as Brendan Rodgers walks through the departure lounge of Palma airport. He scans the information screen, checking the gate number next to EZY8622, the 7.10am flight to London Gatwick. Before long, he is boarding the EasyJet aircraft.

Rodgers places his luggage in an overhead locker and takes a seat near the front of the cabin. He is heading to England's capital on business; for a meeting that will shape the next period of his own career and change the course of Celtic's history.

Over the following days, Rodgers is welcomed into the London home of Dermot Desmond, Celtic's majority shareholder. Out of work after being sacked by Liverpool the previous October, the Northern Irishman has accepted an invitation from Peter Lawwell, the Celtic chief executive, to meet the club's hierarchy and discuss the vacant manager's post. Ronny Deila is in his final week at Celtic and the club plan to make a statement with his successor. They want a manager of class and substance. They want a manager with the vision to create something special and take Celtic forward in Europe. They want Brendan Rodgers.

He listens to Desmond and Lawwell and then asks his own questions. Rodgers is a lifelong Celtic supporter, but that doesn't automatically mean it's the right the club for him. He needs the trust and freedom to run Celtic's football department with autonomy. He has an ambitious long-term plan for the club, but requires the board's backing to achieve his goals. They promise to give him it.

The chemistry between the three men is instant. It is a pivotal meeting, a sliding-doors moment for Celtic and Rodgers. Desmond and Lawwell are hugely impressed. They look into Rodgers' eyes and see a future Celtic manager. They have found their man.

— *London, late May 2016*

SCOTT BROWN'S phone rings. It is a number he doesn't recognise. "Scott, it's Brendan Rodgers. I want us to meet up." Brown is in London on holiday and Rodgers suggests they meet there. The captain is given the address of Rodgers' home in the city

Brown is nervous when he arrives in a taxi but strikes up an instant rapport with the new Celtic manager. Rodgers' fiancée, Charlotte, accepts the gift of a bottle of wine and prepares a meal. Brown and Rodgers retire to another room to talk football. Four hours later, they are still going strong.

The Celtic captain is at a career crossroads as he enters

his tenth year at the club. His 2015/16 season was ravaged by injury. He is about to turn 31 and reports of his demise are widespread, but are they exaggerated? Rodgers is adamant the midfielder is being written off far too early.

His first question to Brown is searching: "How much longer do think you can play at the top level with Celtic?" Brown answers honestly. "Two years. Tops." Rodgers disagrees. "This is a fresh start for you," he says. "Get your fitness right, get your lifestyle and diet right and you can go on until you're 35, at least."

Rodgers explains his plans for Celtic in great detail and outlines exactly where the experienced, long-serving midfielder fits in. He talks about implementing a high-pressing style and his desire to play attacking football with pace and intensity. Brown feels inspired by Rodgers' vision and ambition.

The captain is assured he is crucial to the manager's long-term plans at Celtic. Rodgers tells Brown he believes in him and will support him, but needs dedication and commitment in return. He asks his captain to lead by example and foster a spirit of togetherness in the Celtic squad. The two men embrace as Brown departs. From that first meeting, a close bond is formed.

— *Royal Garden Hotel, Kensington. May 27, 2016*

THE red No.10 double-decker bus bound for King's Cross slows down at the Kensington Palace stop as the car behind takes a sharp left into the forecourt of the Royal Garden Hotel. The driver finds a space in the underground car park and three men emerge from the vehicle.

Moussa Dembele is flanked by agent Mamadi Fofana and his business partner Makan Fofana as he walks into the foyer. It's 10.50am, and the modern hotel on Kensington High Street is busy. The building has a long association with football, having hosted the official reception after England's 1966 World Cup win.

Dembele and his advisors are taken to a private room. Brendan Rodgers is there to greet them. The new Celtic manager shakes the French teenager warmly by the hand and introduces himself to the Fofana cousins.

The 19-year-old is about to leave Fulham. He is a free agent, wanted by some of Europe's biggest clubs. They can offer Dembele more money but Rodgers can provide a platform to progress his career; a clear pathway to become one of the greats. "We can call Luis Suarez and he'll tell you what I can do for you," says the Celtic manager, as he offers the use of his mobile phone.

Dembele considers the Barcelona striker's rise to prominence at Liverpool. His mind is made up by the time the car nudges back out onto Kensington High Street. "Let's make it happen," Dembele tells his agent.

Three days in London. Three lives changed forever. One football club transformed.

INVINCIBLE

PART I: THE INVINCIBLES

— Saturday, May 27, 2017. 2.50pm

NOISE is building inside Hampden Park but a hush descends over the Celtic dressing room. Every member of the squad steps forward from his individual wood-panelled locker. They put their arms around each other's shoulders to form a tight circle. In the middle stands Brendan Rodgers.

They have gone through this ritual before every match this season, but this time it's different. History beckons for this group of Celtic players. Already Premiership Invincibles, they now have the chance to become the first Scottish team to win a Treble without losing a game. Only Aberdeen stand in their way.

Six days earlier, Rodgers stood in the Celtic Park home dressing room before the final league match against

Hearts and urged his team to seize their moment. The Celtic manager wrote the word 'Infrangible' on a board, with a definition underneath: 'To be unbroken, to feel that way.' "Win the game and something very special will follow," Rodgers told them.

Those Celtic players didn't let him down. Goals from Leigh Griffiths and Stuart Armstrong sealed a 2-0 win. Multiple records were shattered at the sound of John Beaton's final whistle as Celtic became the first Scottish team to go through a league season unbeaten since the late 19th century, when it was just an 18-game campaign.

They finish on 106 points, breaking their own 103-point tally from 2001/02 and setting a new European record. Celtic's 34 wins, 106 goals and 30-point winning margin are also historic. "When you look at the past and find out an unbeaten league season was last done in the 1890s, it tells you how difficult it is," said Rodgers. "It's a monumental achievement by the players. I'm not so sure it will happen again in my lifetime."

At Hampden before the Scottish Cup final, Rodgers now stands in the middle of the circle and urges his Celtic team to end a unique season on the ultimate high by lifting the trophy. What follows is a dramatic finale as Tom Rogic's injury-time winner secures the last piece of silverware. "You have to make history – it doesn't just happen," said Rodgers afterwards. "The players showed remarkable courage."

The Celtic manager is given a rapturous reception as he climbs the Hampden steps to hold aloft the Scottish Cup. Legendary status is attained by Rodgers and his players. "It's a monumental achievement," he said. "The players have inscribed their names into the history of this incredible club now. It's something for their kids and grandkids to be proud of. They now stand alone."

Rodgers' team played with panache and invention all season but he also pays tribute to their mentality and focus. "We have had to work hard and earn it," he said. Aberdeen pushed Celtic all the way in the Scottish Cup final, while a dozen Premiership wins came by a single-goal margin. One in particular stood out for Rodgers.

Against Motherwell at Fir Park on December 3, Celtic were 2-0 down at half-time. After drawing level, they trailed 3-2 in the second half but fought back to win the game 4-3 through another Rogic injury-time winner. "It was the first time we'd faced an adverse situation in the league," said Rodgers. "I saw how they coped, stayed calm and went on to dominate. That was a defining moment."

Celtic's Invincible Treble was a triumph for the quality of Rodgers' coaching and man-management skills. Small acts like pushing training back to allow the players to take their kids to their first day at school were a big deal. The monthly training and games calendar given to the squad also allowed them to maximise family time and proved hugely popular.

In a football sense, he improved them all. They became fitter, stronger and more tactically aware. Each time the Celtic team stepped out on the pitch, they were all willing to go the extra yard for Rodgers. Even those who didn't feature, like Kris Commons and Efe Ambrose, spoke of their admiration for the way the Celtic manager had treated them over the course of the season.

Collectively, Celtic were unbeatable. Individually, the awards also poured in. Scott Sinclair won the PFA Scotland and Scottish Football Writers' Association Player of the Year awards, with Scott Brown named as the Ladbrokes Premiership Player of the Year. Kieran Tierney won all three of the Young Player of the Year awards, while Rodgers completed a clean sweep of the Manager of the Year awards. Celtic were Invincible in every sense.

PART II: THE SPIRIT OF '67

THERE has always been a Hollywood element to the Celtic story. In the club's centenary season of 1987/88, Billy McNeill, captain of the Lisbon Lions, masterminded a League and Scottish Cup double as manager. On the 125th anniversary of Celtic being formed in 2012, Barcelona were beaten in the Champions League by Neil Lennon's team, against all the odds.

Going into the 2016/17 season, the achievements of the Lisbon Lions were destined to be a dominant factor, 50 years on from their historic European Cup final win over Inter. Yet Brendan Rodgers' team didn't feel intimidated by the club's past, instead it acted as inspiration.

Gazing up at the spectacular Lisbon Lions tifo that arced around Celtic Park ahead of the final Premiership game, the Celtic players knew they had a chance to write their own unique page in history. They did so by becoming Invincibles and proving that Jock Stein was right when he said Celtic jerseys "don't shrink to fit inferior players". Then, two days after the Lions' 50th anniversary, they honoured the memory further by completing the Treble.

"I was always aware of the Lisbon Lions' story," said Rodgers. "When you think of the football they played, they started the idea of the Celtic Way. Every Celtic team in the future would be judged and measured against that. They were the architects and pioneers of Celtic.

"What they gave us was inspirational and it has been a real fitting season from the 16/17 team. They have played with a lot of the values that the 66/67 team created back then – the spirit, the togetherness, the creativity with the football, the never-say-die attitude and the ability to keep going.

"To go through the season unbeaten is a fitting tribute to them but hopefully the football we have played and our behaviours have also been fitting too. The one thing we can all learn from that era is the humility.

"We've got three values hung up in the changing room which we created before we'd even kicked a ball here: respect, unity and excellence. The definitions of those words are on the wall. People call me modern because I'm young, but I have old-school values. Respect is always the very first one."

PART III: DEMOLITION DERBY

THE Celtic players stand arm in arm in a long line in front of the Broomloan Road stand, soaking up the celebrations. They linger for as long as possible on the Ibrox pitch. It is April 29, 2017 and Celtic have just beaten Rangers 5-1 in a dominant display that illustrates the gulf between the two clubs.

Few wins gave Brendan Rodgers more satisfaction over the course of the 2016/17 season. Rangers had been extremely bullish at the start of the campaign. Fresh from promotion, they unfurled the flag for winning the 2015/16 Scottish Championship and then immediately set their sights on following that up by securing the Premiership title.

Rodgers never publicly commented on this statement of intent initially, but he privately noted the noises coming from the other side of Glasgow. "They obviously thought they could win the league," he later reflected. "The drums were being banged very loudly at the beginning of the season that they were going to win the title, or be the biggest challengers."

The Celtic manager was happy to let Rangers do the talking in that early period. It only reinforced Rodgers' desire to guide his own team to a sixth successive Premiership crown. "We just did our work quietly and prepared the team, focusing on players' development and improvement," he said.

After Celtic's 5-1 win in late April, his low-key approach was vindicated. It was a dominant performance from Rodgers' team in the club's biggest victory at Ibrox since 1897. The winning margin would have been even greater had Celtic not missed a host of chances in both halves. "It could have been close to double figures," said Mikael Lustig.

Celtic finished that day 36 points ahead of Rangers. They had 18 shots at goal in a match that hammered home their superiority. That was Rodgers' aim before kick-off. "In terms of these games, I don't think it matters if it's zero points, one point or 33 points of a gap," he said. "You're playing for pride, you're defending the culture of your club."

The gulf between the two teams was stark. Celtic's performance was far superior to the 5-1 home win over Rangers in September. "There's a totally different dynamic to the team," said Rodgers. "When I came in my job was to build a team who could go into any stadium without fear and play. This is one of the great rivals for Celtic, so for us to come to Ibrox and show that was pleasing."

Celtic's personnel at Ibrox on April 29 demonstrated the transformational effect Rodgers had on his players over the course of the season. Scott Sinclair and Eboue Kouassi, for 10 seconds, were the only new signings to feature. With Moussa Dembele injured, every other player involved in the game had been inherited by Rodgers. They had also been reborn.

The Celtic team was unrecognisable from the previous season. The composure of Craig Gordon, the strength and solidity of Dedryck Boyata and Jozo Simunovic, and the sharpness of Lustig and Kieran Tierney gave Celtic a platform to win the game. In midfield, Scott Brown was in total control. Next to him, Callum McGregor and Stuart Armstrong were perpetual motion. In attack, the pace and invention of Sinclair and Patrick Roberts complemented Leigh Griffiths' devilish display.

Celtic showed why they were Premiership champions that day at Ibrox. The early-season noise from their neighbours had been silenced. A few hours after the victory, captain Brown took to Instagram to thank the Celtic fans for their support. He signed off his post with a simple message: "Glasgow's green and white."

PART IV: DEATH BY FOOTBALL

BRENDAN RODGERS was hosting a Q&A with Liverpool fans in September 2012 when he delivered the following insight into his preference for a possession-based game. "When you've got the ball 65 to 70 per cent of the time, it's a football death for the other team," he said. "It's death by football."

Up and down Scotland, opposition managers will understand exactly what Rodgers meant by this statement. Rival players refer to "the grind" of playing against Celtic. When the Premiership champions are in possession, they pull their opponents all over the place, moving the ball back and forward, or from side to side, constantly probing for openings.

If there is no space, Celtic are content to recycle possession all the way back to Craig Gordon before building again. They just keep chipping away, knowing they will break through eventually. It's an energy-sapping style of play to go up against. Legs tire as the game progresses, mistakes are made and space opens up. Celtic are relentless and ruthless.

When out of possession, they work even harder. Rodgers tells his players to "defend forward" and be aggressive when they lose the ball. He often refers to the importance of their "counter-press". When Celtic lose the ball, they don't automatically fall back into a defensive set-up and let the other team build. They press hard and high, with intelligence, to go and win it back again immediately.

Two goals late in the 2016/17 campaign illustrated their relentless drive and desire. In the 5-1 win over Rangers at Ibrox on April 29, Kieran Tierney lost possession inside the opponent's half. Yet Pedro Caixinha's team didn't even complete one pass before Celtic won the ball back again. Mikael Lustig nipped in ahead of Kenny Miller and his jinking run ended with a composed finish for Celtic's fifth goal.

One week later, Celtic's aggressive counter-pressing again shone in the 4-1 win over St Johnstone. Tommy Wright's team were forced back deep in their half and when Joe Shaughnessy tried to play a pass into midfield, Callum McGregor was there to intercept and embarked on a slaloming sprint into the box before scoring.

That goal came in the 71st minute. Lustig's against Rangers was clocked at 87 minutes. Late strikes in games were a recurring theme over the course of the season as Celtic's relentless probing and pressing left opponents shattered. Over 41 per cent of their 106 Premiership goals – 44 – came in the last half hour of games. A staggering 26.4 per cent – 28 – came in the final 15 minutes.

It was the same in the cup competitions. In the Scottish Cup, six of Celtic's 17 goals came in the last 15 minutes, including Tom Rogic's injury-time winner against Aberdeen in the final to seal the Treble. In the Betfred Cup, four of Celtic's goals came during that late period. Moussa Dembele's dramatic semi-final winner against Rangers was the most important of them all.

"We always want to circulate the ball and get teams moving," said McGregor. "But if it breaks down then we try and hunt it back as quickly as we can. That can demoralise teams as they think, 'Here we go, we have to try to get it back again'. Our mindset is that as soon as we lose it we want to get it straight back. It just tires teams out. We are grinding them down all the time.

"We keep going and keep being relentless and that's when the fitness side of things comes into it. At the end of a game we still have the quality, the fitness and the mental sharpness to make the right decisions at the right time. This is the fittest I've felt as a player, but the mental fitness is so important too."

For Rodgers, this marriage of physical and mental strength was key to Celtic's Invincible season. "The ability to know that when others are flagging you can keep going is a huge thing to have in your armoury," he said. "You have to keep demanding. It would be easy at 3-1 or 4-1 up just to sit off, but no. You have to keep going right to the very end and keep pushing."

PART V: THE HOLY TRINITY

'EMPTY jerseys, empty hearts, empty dreams, empty stands' was the message emblazoned on one banner from the Celtic supporters. 'You've embarrassed yourselves' said another, while claiming 'The Celtic jersey has shrunk to fit inferior players'.

It was Sunday, April 24, 2016. One week on from Celtic's Scottish Cup semi-final defeat by Rangers and the fans made their displeasure known. Dermot Desmond, Celtic's majority shareholder, and Peter Lawwell, the club's chief executive, were both name-checked in this public display of discontent.

Ronny Deila's broken team drew 1-1 with Ross County that day. It was a listless performance and by then the Norwegian's departure was already announced. Desmond and Lawwell would soon begin their bid to bring Rodgers on board as manager. Just over four weeks later, he was appointed. The Celtic fans got the change they wanted.

From day one, Rodgers galvanised the Celtic support. Over 13,000 turned up to see him paraded on May 23. Queues snaked around the Celtic Park ticket office for season tickets over the next few weeks. Sales soared to over 50,000 again. The following March, the club announced a waiting list for the 2017/18 season tickets. It was the first time that had happened since the Martin O'Neill era.

"My idea is to get the stands full again," said Rodgers at his unveiling. "In the last few years, the top tier of the Lisbon Lions stand has been closed. It is my job to get 60,000 fans in here and inspire supporters to get back."

The Celtic manager succeeded. After a period of

falling attendances, Celtic Park was packed on a weekly basis. Rodgers transformed the club. His appointment was a masterstroke from Desmond and Lawwell as the supporters developed a close connection and bond with the manager and his players, many of whom had been written off at the end of the previous season.

After every game, home and away, Rodgers made a point of ensuring the Celtic players thanked the fans for their support. Following the 3-1 over Aberdeen on May 12, he instructed his entire squad to throw their Celtic jerseys into the Pittodrie away end to give kids a souvenir.

The day Celtic became Premiership Invincibles began with the team being dropped off at the bottom of the Celtic Way, some 90 minutes before the game started. Fans lined the walkway as Rodgers and his players strode up towards the stadium, soaking up the acclaim and thanking the crowd for their support.

Following the trophy presentation, the celebrations ended with Kieran Tierney holding a loudhailer as he led the Celtic supporters in a chant. Similarly, the jubilant scenes sparked by Tom Rogic's Scottish Cup winner entered club folklore. The bond between pitch and stand had been broken 12 months earlier. Now it had never been stronger.

"With the Celtic I know, the strength has always been being together," said Rodgers. "What we have proven this year is the fusion between the players, the management and the supporters. When that's together, Celtic is a powerful force.

"There will be bumps along the way in the journey, but if that Holy Trinity can stay together, then we can achieve and give them happiness. I know what makes them happy and I will do everything I can to bring them that."

ONE VISION, ONE CLUB

THE official job title was first-team manager but, in reality, Celtic were searching for a football architect; a top-quality coach with vision, ambition and drive. In Brendan Rodgers, they found the perfect candidate.

The former Liverpool manager was relaxed about his future when he walked through the front door of Dermot Desmond's London home in early May 2016. He had agreed to meet Celtic's majority shareholder and Peter Lawwell, the club's chief executive, for talks, partly out of courtesy, but mostly intrigue.

This wasn't a job interview as such. Rodgers was determined to return to management that summer and wondered if Celtic could match his ambitions. Across the table, the club's two key decision-makers were similarly curious as they targeted a box-office appointment following the departure of Ronny Deila.

What followed was a meeting of minds. Rodgers listened intently to the pitch from Desmond and Lawwell and liked what he heard. He was given assurances that resources would be available to strengthen the squad, and the passion from the two men impressed him as he asked searching questions about Celtic's future and the direction in which the club wanted to travel.

Rodgers was interested to find out if Celtic were content to simply qualify for the Champions League group stages, or if they had ambitions to become regulars in the tournament's knockout rounds. The Celtic hierarchy were honest in their answers as they mapped out their plans. They couldn't match the European superpowers' finance but they wanted to create a club that could consistently compete at the highest level. Celtic weren't content to just make up the numbers.

When Rodgers shook hands and walked out of that initial discussion, he began to seriously ponder whether he should relaunch his managerial career in Glasgow. Celtic, a club he had supported all his life, represented an attractive opportunity for him at the age of 43.

During a January 2016 Sky Sports interview, Rodgers spoke about a desire to win trophies at his next club. "No matter where you go, what country it is, you want to be in with a chance of winning," he said. Celtic offered him that chance and much more. It was time to take stock and weigh up his options.

"Peter rang me when Ronny announced he was going to leave," explained Rodgers. "I'm a Celtic supporter, I love the club, so out of respect, I thought I would go and speak to both Peter and Dermot. I came to see whether I could help the club.

"I was quite open-minded. There was no pressure either way. I was interested to hear about Celtic. I could see the hunger and the passion in Dermot's eyes. He wasn't just talking through any old spiel to get me here."

The emotional pull for Rodgers could not be underestimated. He had been steeped in Celtic from an early age, growing up as a supporter of the club. Family members continued to make the pilgrimage from their home village of Carnlough, Northern Ireland, to Celtic Park regularly, just like they had for decades. As a kid, he often joined them.

Rodgers couldn't let his heart rule his head, though. He had to make this decision for the benefit of his career. The new Celtic manager's remit would be wide and varied but there were three key tasks: maintain the club's domination of Scottish football, make progress on the European scene and continue the successful, profitable development of young talent.

After a period of reflection, Rodgers realised Celtic ticked a lot of boxes. They didn't have the endless millions that the giants of the English game boasted but this was a massive, familiar club in a football-mad city. There were obvious pitfalls. The Scottish Premiership's lowly ranking meant that domestic dominance alone wouldn't be enough to enhance Rodgers' reputation. European success held the key in this regard but that challenge excited him.

Rodgers considered the negatives but still felt the job perfectly suited his ambitions and strengths. Factor in his affinity with Celtic and it was ideal. He would have the opportunity to win silverware, create new history and possibly manage in the Champions League group stages. At Chelsea, Swansea and Liverpool, he proved adept at nurturing precocious youngsters. He would be given the licence to do the same at Celtic, working with the best local talent and foreign imports.

Yet what Celtic offered Rodgers more than anything was freedom. Towards the end of his Liverpool reign, he appeared to be hampered by the 'transfer committee' system utilised by the Anfield owners. Players he didn't necessarily want, like Mario Balotelli, were foisted upon him.

There would be no such problems at Celtic. Rodgers was told he would assume control of the entire football operation and was promised the financial backing to take it forward. That level of control was crucial. Desmond was willing to give him the freedom to create something special and, crucially, implement all the key components of Rodgers' own 'One Vision, One Club' football blueprint.

"The people at Celtic gave me total trust and that can't be underestimated," said Rodgers. "All the experience I have had from being a youth coach to a manager, I'd now be able to impose. Liverpool was an incredible club, but complicated. I struggled in that environment. I need a level of control to allow me to function."

'One Vision, One Club' is Rodgers' life's work. Almost 200 pages in length, it has been crafted over two decades, with the latest version updated and revised to take in the contrasting experiences of his Liverpool reign. He would eventually hand a copy of this document to Desmond, Lawwell and every Celtic director.

Its contents detail everything from his favoured style of play to the type of players he wants to work with, from personality to ability, and the high standards he expects them to reach. "It's not the right or wrong way – it's my way," said Rodgers, in reference to 'One Vision, One Club'. "I want to be decisive and clear about how I work. Then if people want to employ me they will understand how I work.

"I started it when I began coaching. Over the years,

I pulled it all into a format. Then I suppose you create a brand for yourself that people understand and recognise. I loved the experience of pulling it together."

Rodgers was always top of Celtic's wish-list from the moment it was announced Deila was leaving on April 20, but the club did have other candidates for the job. Former Celtic player David Moyes, then out of work, was of interest, but made it clear he preferred to wait for a job in England. Northern Ireland's Michael O'Neill and former Celtic manager Neil Lennon were two other strong contenders for the vacancy.

The club spoke to "in excess of six" candidates according to Lawwell, but Rodgers quickly became Celtic's preferred choice. Desmond, an Irish businessman who has made billions from successfully sealing deals throughout his career, was convinced he was the right man and upped the ante just as Rodgers was weighing up the prospect of becoming Celtic manager during a pivotal period in May.

"Dermot made a couple of really important calls to me after we met," said Rodgers. "We had a real long conversation one night on the phone. He made it pretty clear that I was the one they wanted at Celtic."

It was easy to understand why Rodgers fitted the bill for Desmond and Lawwell. He was young and hungry to succeed. He understood Celtic and had the experience of handling the pressure at Liverpool. His track record of developing young players suited Celtic, who had brought in millions from selling the likes of Virgil van Dijk and Victor Wanyama to England after identifying them and providing a European platform on which to flourish.

The supporters would also embrace the appointment. Rodgers had a reputation for building attractive teams with a dynamic, attacking style and would play the traditional Celtic Way. There was a belief he would put thousands more bums on seats at Celtic Park and allow the club's fanbase to regain a sense of excitement after the disappointing end to Deila's reign.

Celtic had won five successive titles under Lennon and Deila but the final season of the Norwegian's tenure, and the absence of Champions League football for two seasons, had led to a disconnect between the supporters and board. To borrow a quote from Lennon, Celtic needed someone to "bring the thunder back".

The board felt Rodgers would do that and Desmond was prepared to sanction a staggering financial package in excess of £2million per annum to get his man. This was over three times what Deila earned. Wages would not be an issue in attracting a manager of Rodgers' calibre. He conducts his own deals without an agent and was assured that Celtic were willing to pay the going rate of a Premier League salary.

Celtic's only fear was that the move would be scuppered by the understandable lure of English football. Rodgers had already turned down three offers from the Premier League and the next one wouldn't be far away. The unappealing prospect of six difficult, season-defining Champions League qualifiers over the summer, with a squad needing an injection of quality and confidence, was another negative factor.

Football figures were queuing up to offer Rodgers advice as he neared a decision and several told him he would be making a mistake in joining Celtic "I had a number of guys who said 'Don't go. Why would you go?'" he later admitted. The standard of Scottish football and the perceived lack of competition meant that, within the wider football community, it was viewed as a step down for Rodgers. Even Michael O'Neill admitted he was a "little surprised" that his fellow Northern Irishman was considering Celtic.

Ultimately, though, Rodgers wanted something new, a fresh challenge in a different environment. He wanted a project that would stimulate and excite him. Celtic were completely dominant in Scotland but he could see potential for improvement, particularly in a European sense. Champions League qualification would be difficult but not impossible.

After weighing everything up, Rodgers officially accepted Celtic's offer on May 20 and became the highest-paid manager in the club's history. He was in Majorca when the paperwork was signed and celebrated with fiancée Charlotte, toasting the news with a glass of champagne as they looked across Port Adriano. Rodgers was formally unveiled three days later on a one-year rolling contract. It was a major coup for the Celtic board, the biggest since Martin O'Neill was appointed in 2000, and a massive statement of intent ahead of the new season.

"Dermot asked me to be the architect of the club and create something," said Rodgers. "This wasn't a decision purely on emotion, it was going to be about a professional move. When I spoke to the people at the club, they sold it to me. It was too good an opportunity to turn down. I never knew if it would come again. I only came to Scotland for Celtic. I grew up a supporter and understand the ethos and the values. It's an iconic club worldwide. I think it was fate really that got me to Celtic. The timing just happened to be perfect. I was fed up taking holidays, I was ready to work."

Throughout the British game, there was surprise that Rodgers could be tempted to Celtic at such a relatively young age. At his peak, as manager of a flamboyant Liverpool team, just two years earlier, even he would never have imagined Scottish football being his next port of call.

Rodgers' star was on the rise in season 2013/14, with the Anfield club on the verge of winning the Premier League. Liverpool had won 11 consecutive games going into the final three fixtures and needed seven points to guarantee a first title since 1990. Then Steven Gerrard infamously slipped in a defeat by Chelsea and the initiative was handed to Manchester City. Liverpool never recovered.

Yet the plaudits still rolled in for Rodgers. With Luis Suarez in unstoppable form, Liverpool had scored 101 Premier League goals as they finished in second place and it felt like the start of an exciting era at Anfield. Rodgers won the LMA Manager of the Year award and signed a new four-year contract at the club.

Retaining Suarez was key to Liverpool's hopes of building on the 2013/14 season but that proved to be impossible. Even a four-month ban for biting Italy's Giorgio Chiellini during a World Cup match didn't deter Barcelona from striking a £75million deal to take the Uruguayan forward to La Liga on July 11, 2014.

Without their talisman, Liverpool finished sixth in the Premier League the following season and reached two domestic semi-finals. But by October 2015, after a poor start to the league campaign, Rodgers was under mounting pressure and was eventually sacked and replaced by Jurgen Klopp. It had been a rollercoaster period but despite the way it ended, Rodgers remained a respected, coveted coach in the English game.

By February 2016, five months after leaving Liverpool, he disclosed in a beIN Sports interview that he had rejected several job offers, including at least three in the

Premier League. Rodgers was content to wait until that summer for a new challenge and stressed that he wanted something that would "excite" him.

Rodgers conceded that his career had taken an unexpected detour to bring him to Glasgow but given his attachment to the club, he wondered whether it was all somehow meant to be. "I think it was fate really that got me to Celtic," he said. "So many stars have aligned for me to be here at this time. The most important thing was the challenge and to work somewhere different.

"I'd five years in the Premier League with Swansea and Liverpool and that's great. I loved my time there. If I've another 20 years of management in me then I was never always going to be in the Premier League. I would never want that. I'm here now at Celtic, a club I love and a team I want to do well with and also got an affinity for. That's what excites me.

"I could have come back to the Premier League, but to be at Celtic is a huge privilege. This is an iconic club, one that expects to win titles and to also be competitive in Europe. The measure will be on both of those and that's what I'm driven to achieve.

"I took time out after Liverpool to reflect and I needed to ensure when I came back, it wasn't for one or two seasons. My intention is to be at Celtic for as long as I possibly can, to let the club grow and to take it as far as I can. For me, it's about enjoying my life. I'm living the dream being the manager of Celtic ."

MORE THAN A JOB

MAY 23, 2016. Brendan Rodgers pauses for a second as he strolls through a narrow corridor deep inside Celtic Park on his way to greet the club's supporters for the first time. A door is being held open for the new manager but a framed image on the wall catches his eye.

It is an old Celtic squad photo from the 1986/87 season and Rodgers smiles as he picks out several familiar faces. The iconic beard of Danny McGrain is there, as is Tommy Burns' shock of red hair. Paul McStay adds an air of understated class with a haircut as tidy as any of the measured passes he played on the pitch that Rodgers will soon step onto.

These Celtic legends were his heroes growing up; players who shaped his love of football. In that moment, Rodgers was transported back to the 1980s and his home town of Carnlough, a seaside village in County Antrim, Northern Ireland.

It was there he developed his skills as a kid playing on

the grass behind St John's Primary school, dreaming of one day starring for Celtic. He idolised McStay and Burns, who would become a mentor for him in his formative coaching days at Reading in the 1990s.

An hour or so later, Rodgers recalled his first-ever Celtic game in impressive detail. It was a 1984 pre-season friendly against Finn Harps in a little town called Ballybofey, across the Republic of Ireland border in County Donegal. "I was 11," smiled Rodgers. "My uncles and cousins started me off from my early years."

These Celtic memories and this familiarity with a club he was brought up with in Carnlough was a major reason why Rodgers was persuaded to take on a position he described as "more than a job" on that first day in May. He understood the fabric of Celtic and wanted to be part of the history.

"This is different," he said. "This is family, this is blood, this is Patsy Gallacher, Jimmy Johnstone, Danny McGrain. It's more than a job and it's more than a club. It's a way of life for people. I want to help make their days better and make them proud of their team."

Burns, who passed away after a battle with cancer in 2008, was Reading manager when Rodgers was setting out on his coaching career at the English club. He gave him huge encouragement and they developed an enduring friendship. Rodgers recalled how Burns talked to him at length about the prospect of one day working together at Celtic, with Burns as director of football and Rodgers as first-team coach.

That was Burns' long-term vision. Through tragic circumstances, the dream Celtic management team they spoke about never materialised. Yet his close friend was uppermost in Rodgers' thoughts on the day of his unveiling. "I think Tommy would be proud," he said. It was also fitting that Jonathan Burns, Tommy's son, was in the Celtic Park boardroom to congratulate the new manager.

Rodgers made the journey from Carnlough to Celtic Park many times as a schoolboy. He recalled joining his uncles and cousins on the ferry over the Irish Sea, stopping at Baird's Bar on the Gallowgate en route to Celtic Park. They were 13-hour days, starting and ending with the 15-mile journey between Carnlough and Larne.

"We'd be there at 8am every second Saturday to get the boat to Stranraer then up to Celtic Park," said Kieran McMullan, Rodgers' cousin. "We'd be back in Carnlough by 9pm, so it would be a 13-hour trip to see Celtic but we all loved it. Brendan is eight years younger me, so I'd have to look after him but that wasn't a problem. I was the senior boy on most of the trips but he was always a good kid."

THREE decades on from those childhood trips to Celtic Park, Rodgers was back, this time for his unveiling as the club's new manager. Celtic marketed it as the start of the Rodgers Revolution and what transpired was a day that will live with him forever.

It was after lunchtime when the private jet from London to Glasgow touched down at the city's airport. He was met by Celtic officials and taken to One Devonshire Gardens, an elite West End hotel, where he changed into a suit after checking in. The waiting grey Mercedes people carrier then took him on towards the stadium, where thousands of fans were already there to greet him.

At exactly 3.30pm, Rodgers' vehicle turned left at the Celtic Way and began the slow drive up to the front entrance. Supporters lined the road but it became apparent that a lot more were on their way. Something unique was taking place. Celtic staff scrambled to open up the main stand's turnstiles as the appointment got an immediate endorsement from the fans.

Rodgers met senior Celtic officials and board members in the boardroom and then conducted around two hours of media duties. Peter Lawwell, Celtic's chief executive, introduced him as a "special manager" as Sky Sports News beamed the press conference live from Celtic Park's Number 7 restaurant.

By 6.05pm, Celtic Park's main stand was packed and lower sections of the Jock Stein and Lisbon Lions stands also had to be opened. It was estimated that 13,000 supporters were there to welcome Rodgers on his first day as the Celtic manager.

"It's an incredible turnout but I can't say I'm surprised," he said, speaking from a podium on the pitch while wearing a green and white scarf. "Celtic supporters never fail to support their men. I'll never forget Tommy Burns saying to me, 'When you become the Celtic manager, Brendan, you are a leader of the men and a leader of the people'. I'm very proud to be here, so thank you very much."

Rodgers' words led to a euphoric roar and standing ovation. He was still shaking hands outside the stadium an hour later as fans waited to catch a glimpse of him. This welcome had a huge impact on the new Celtic manager, who was told season ticket queues were longer than they had been in a decade. It only heightened his determination to give the supporters a team to be proud of.

"As we were travelling to Celtic Park, I was told, 'Listen,

we have to open up the stadium," said Rodgers. "So to walk out to that for an unveiling was really special — something that will live with me for the rest of my life. I was thinking, 'Right, what am I going to say here?', but it was the most beautiful day. I will never forget walking out for the first time."

Leigh Griffiths was the only Celtic player present on his first day but the appointment was universally welcomed by the squad Rodgers inherited. It was the hot topic in the WhatsApp group chat used by the players and there was renewed excitement and optimism about the season ahead.

Previous manager Deila had been far from unpopular. The Celtic players respected him and he had played a major role in developing the careers of players like Griffiths, Kieran Tierney and Tom Rogic. Yet, the overwhelming belief was that Rodgers, after his work at Swansea and Liverpool, would take Celtic to a different level.

Speaking on international duty with Sweden, Mikael Lustig, a senior member of the Celtic squad, made it clear that he expected Rodgers to have far more influence and clout than Deila. "In the last few years we haven't signed anyone who comes with such hype," said Lustig. "This shows we are really going for it."

Even Deila disclosed that Rodgers was an upgrade on his own appointment. The Norwegian knew his time was up after the Scottish Cup semi-final defeat by Rangers and had no issue with standing aside. "This is a fantastic choice for Celtic, they couldn't have picked a better manager than Brendan," said Deila. "I am very happy with the news. He will lead the club to the heights they should be at."

That was Rodgers' plan but he couldn't do it all by

himself. The Celtic manager is never slow to acknowledge the importance of a strong support staff and made plans to bring in fresh talent to augment the qualities possessed by the club's existing backroom team.

Chris Davies, Rodgers' former youth-team captain at Reading, had worked with him at Swansea and Liverpool and was appointed as Celtic's new assistant manager. Like Rodgers, Davies turned to coaching at an early age after injury curtailed his playing career. A Loughborough University graduate in sports science, 31-year-old Davies was regarded as a progressive coach of undoubted promise and held in high regard within English football.

He had been operating as assistant manager at Reading but immediately accepted Rodgers' invitation to join him. Davies regarded the new Celtic manager as the biggest influence on his career. "Brendan has been a mentor to me," he said. "He was a great coach to me as a player and even when I had to stop, Brendan told me there was still a big career for me in football."

Davies had a reputation for being strong on the tactical, strategic side of the game, having worked as an opposition analyst at Liverpool. Armed with a bubbly, confident personality, he had also developed close relationships with key players like Jordan Henderson at Liverpool. Rodgers placed great faith in his natural ability to connect with the Celtic squad, individually and collectively, and get the maximum performance levels out of them.

Glen Driscoll was another key recruit as Celtic's new head of performance. He too had previously worked with Rodgers at Chelsea, Swansea and Liverpool. Driscoll was given responsibility for overseeing the conditioning and fitness work at the club, and worked closely with medical staff in the key areas of injury prevention and rehabilitation to ensure player availability levels were as high as possible. By October, Jack Nayler had also been recruited as Celtic's head of sports science, working alongside John Currie and the other fitness staff. The grandson of former Tottenham Hotspur manager Keith Burkinshaw, Nayler had an impressive CV, which included stints at Chelsea, PSG and Real Madrid, where he'd been part of a Champions League-winning backroom team under Carlo Ancelotti.

Yet Rodgers was keen to work with Celtic's existing staff and John Kennedy continued in his role as first-team coach. He was another whose playing career had been cut short through injury, but had worked in several coaching and scouting roles within Celtic after retiring and was held in the highest esteem within the dressing room.

Stevie Woods, Celtic's goalkeeping coach, also quickly became an integral part of Rodgers' backroom team. He had helped make Fraser Forster an England internationalist and was also key to Craig Gordon's unlikely comeback.

Rodgers had vowed to "look within the club" when filling other positions and moved John McGlynn to become more involved in analysing opponents. The former Hearts manager had been working as a first-team scout but Rodgers felt his skills and knowledge of the Scottish and European game could be invaluable when preparing for fixtures at home and abroad.

With the basis of his backroom team finalised in late May, Rodgers focused more on his squad and continued to analyse the strengths and weakness. He also spoke to players individually, phoning several and meeting captain Scott Brown in London for a lengthy conversation on the season ahead.

Rodgers had made a point of highlighting the Celtic midfielder's importance during his opening media briefings. Brown was told he would retain the armband and was invited to his new manager's home in the English capital to discuss Rodgers' plans for the season ahead and allow him to outline exactly what he expected from his on-field leader.

"We were able to meet up and have a really good chat," said Rodgers. "Scott's been here a long time. He's been through the good times and the tough times, so it was good to get his opinion on how things are and how it looks for him at the club, as well as giving me the opportunity to introduce myself to him as the club captain and talk through my ideas and how I'd like to work."

It was a hectic early period for Rodgers but he had little time to waste. The Champions League qualifiers started on July 12, just seven weeks after he was appointed. The work to ensure Celtic reached the group stages had already begun.

LOS DETALLITOS

THE Habakuk Hotel sits at the bottom of the picturesque Pohorje mountains, on the outskirts of Maribor city centre in Slovenia. A sprawling four-star complex, it specialises in sports training camps and winter ski holidays. The Habakuk had been identified by Celtic as a potential summer pre-season base in early 2016 and was then rubber-stamped by Brendan Rodgers after his arrival. It was there, in the lush, green Slovenian countryside that the new manager would properly get to work.

Celtic's journey to Maribor was far from straightforward. The club's charter flight, on June 27, 2016, was 30 minutes away from landing at the city airport when the pilot suddenly announced an unscheduled detour to Zagreb, the Croatian capital.

The Celtic party had been delayed when leaving

Glasgow but the Maribor airport officials made no special allowances for their VIP guests. They clocked off for the night and forced the plane to land in the neighbouring country, 116 kilometres away.

It was a bizarre start to the trip but Rodgers didn't let his displeasure show in public, doing his utmost to play down the impact of the disruption. The players gathered in a deserted airport cafe to watch the first half of England's shock defeat to Iceland at Euro 2016, while an emergency bus was scrambled to pick them up.

When Celtic set off on the two-hour, cross-border coach journey to their Maribor base, captain Scott Brown and his team-mates were huddled around laptops and tablets to take in the final moments of an incredible Icelandic victory in Nice. By the time they reached the hotel after a long day of travelling, it was well past midnight.

The players needed their rest as training was intense in the searing Slovenian summer heat. At first, Celtic worked on a single pitch at the bottom of a valley on the edge of the hotel grounds. Privacy was an issue, however, as other teams trained on adjacent surfaces and within days of arriving, Celtic relocated to the nearby home of a semi-professional club.

It was a modest, tranquil setting in a sleepy village and Rodgers was satisfied as he gradually increased the demands. Double sessions were the norm, with team meetings a daily occurrence. Physically and mentally, it was a gruelling period for the players. They were being pushed and tested constantly.

Rodgers places huge value on the importance of clear, concise communication. He views it as a key asset for any successful football coach and used the bulk of his time in Maribor to get ideas across and spend more time interacting with his new players. "The quality of your life is down to the quality of your communication skills," he said.

During training and in and around the hotel, through analysis sessions and one-to-one meetings, the Celtic manager took advantage of any chance to get inside his players' heads. He made a point of spending time with every member of his squad.

"I'm pretty sure their brains will be sore," said Rodgers, after the first fortnight of pre-season training. "We're piling a lot of work into them so they're having to digest a lot, on and off the field. There are double sessions, review sessions, analysis of performance. So there is a lot of work going in, but they're taking the concepts on board really well.

"If you want to be the best player you can be, then you've got to be a thinker. We have been talking about having 11 players in the team but having one brain. You've got to think about the game, think about every element of football. You play the game with your brain and I like players to have that intelligence to problem solve."

The Celtic squad and staff got to know more about Rodgers' high standards and demands in Maribor. Every training session was planned in the minute detail. Celtic players put in the miles of hard running as they worked on increasing their base fitness, but it was also a modern pre-season training schedule in every sense.

The drills were varied and almost all involved ball-work. Rodgers explained to his players exactly what he expected before every session and the intensity never dropped, from the *rondos* to the small-sided, match-specific possession games and technical sprinting and passing exercises. Rodgers demanded a team with the capability to press relentlessly at pace during games and his players worked on making explosive five-yard bursts at different angles after fast-feet exercises.

The backroom staff Rodgers inherited worked harder than ever but, to a man, were hugely impressed. Hours were long but they saw that Rodgers was not afraid to put in a shift himself. John Kennedy, who had served as a coach under Neil Lennon and Ronny Deila, spoke openly about the ways in which the new manager had taken every aspect of Celtic's preparations up a notch.

"He is very precise," said Kennedy. "Even for a meeting or a training session, it's all done to the last detail. The colours of the cones and the poles have to match and the pitch has to look a certain way when we go out. Even down to session plans, there are red and green pens for different teams. But we are a top club and we need to have top standards."

Rodgers' attention to detail even extended to every member of the Celtic travelling party – from the chef to club media – wearing colour-coordinated kit each day. The team was sponsored by New Balance, and the manager didn't want to see a mix of manufacturers and logos worn by those representing the club, in whatever capacity. "We are all unified," he said.

The work was relentless but the new manager also understood the importance of downtime for his players. He treated them as adults and booked out a Maribor city centre hotel for a team meal and bonding night in the second week. This allowed players and staff to unwind before pre-season training stepped up a gear again.

Rodgers' aim was to put his long-term vision and short-term ambitions across to his players. On day four of the Slovenia trip, he gathered the squad together and reminded them that the Champions League group stage draw was exactly eight weeks away. Rodgers settled on specific targets with his players for the season ahead. These included 100 league goals, a clean sweep of domestic trophies and an unbeaten home record, all of which were achieved. However, the priority, above everything else, was to negotiate the three rounds of qualifiers and reach the group stages of Europe's elite club competition for the first time in three years. "We have to find a way," Rodgers told his players.

The Celtic manager also put his ideas down in black and white, with every member of the squad handed a detailed dossier on his football philosophy and what they could expect working under him. A training and fixture schedule spanning the next two months was included. Each player was asked to read the document, digest it and come back with any questions.

"It was just a snapshot of what I expect," said Rodgers. "Players learn in different ways. Some will learn on the field, some will learn visually by looking at videos and some learn by reading.

"What I provide is the different ways of learning. The document is based on a welcome to the club, a personal letter from me. Players get a monthly calendar so they know exactly what their schedule is. It is not a daily thing.

"They get the fundamentals of how we play in terms of offensive organisation, defensive organisation, offensive transition, defensive transition. Then they get the rules and regulations of how I work. From relationships with people, to turning up late.

"It's a document that outlines the parameters of how we work and gives them ideas. It's a watered-down version of what I give the senior directors and the senior staff at the club. That was a full document of my scheme of work.

"I bring that into every club and then adapt it to the club. People then understand straight away. It's details. Or as they say in Spain, los detallitos... the small details.

"Uniform is unity. If everyone is uniformed and you have a way of working then everyone feels part of it. You then see the magic begin and over time it evolves in front of you. It's great. It takes time but you put it in place at the beginning, you see it develop and it's beautiful."

Pre-season friendlies are rarely easy on the eye. They are merely a necessary evil. Celtic played three Slovenian teams – Celje, Olimpija Ljubljana and Maribor – during their tour and also made a trip across the border to beat Austrian club Sturm Graz. Those games were a chance for Rodgers to improve fitness, work on different formations and take a closer look at around 30 players.

Celtic mostly switched between a 4-3-3 system and the 4-2-3-1 formation favoured by Deila. Given the importance of the upcoming qualifiers, Rodgers was wary of changing too much, too soon in terms of tactics. "This trip is about football fitness and mental fitness more than anything else," he said.

A 2-2 draw with Celje was followed by 1-0 and 2-1 wins over Graz and Olimpija respectively. The trip was rounded off with a feisty 0-0 stalemate with Maribor. It was during this match that the Celtic squad discovered Rodgers would fight their corner.

Leigh Griffiths was spat on by Maribor left-back Erik Janza during the first half and the Celtic manager didn't hold back afterwards. "It was a disgraceful act," said Rodgers, as Maribor officials stared uneasily at the floor. His willingness to speak up on their behalf did not go unnoticed by the Celtic players.

That was an unfortunate end to the trip but the Slovenian football community had been excited by Rodgers' presence. Every coach in the top division requested access to watch a Celtic training session and government officials were also granted an audience. Rodgers made time for them and ensured his players gave the local media interviews as he thanked the Slovenian people for hosting the club.

The only brief distraction came in the days following Roy Hodgson's resignation as England manager. It is well known that Rodgers has admirers within the FA and he was immediately installed as one of the early favourites to replace Hodgson, despite having not taken charge of a Celtic game at that point. His reaction was to laugh off the speculation.

"I haven't put a foot wrong here... brilliant," Rodgers smiled. "I've just landed my dream job. The team I've supported all my life. I haven't even had my first game. Imagine me as a Celtic fan having walked out on the job at Parkhead? I'll be at Celtic, that's for sure."

As always, dedicated Celtic supporters travelled to each friendly and the new manager made a point of acknowledging their backing. Before the game in Graz, he wandered across the pitch and spent five minutes chatting with the group of diehard fans in the far corner of the modern UPC-Arena and thanking them for their support.

It was a small gesture but a big thing for those supporters, who returned home with their selfies and memories. "Are we signing Kolo Toure," one shouted to Rodgers as he said goodbye. "We'll see," smiled the Celtic manager knowingly.

The first new signing did arrive in Slovenia. Moussa

Dembele, an outstanding teenage French striking prospect, joined from Fulham for around £500,000 in what was a major coup for Celtic. Rodgers, though, had little time to bed him in, with the first Champions League qualifier scheduled for the second week in July. Celtic expected to play Flora Tallinn but the Estonians were shocked over two legs by Lincoln Red Imps from Gibraltar.

The manager got that news just minutes after Celtic had beaten Olimpija Ljubljana in the Slovenian capital and his immediate concern was that the team would be in action 24 hours earlier than expected. This development got him thinking.

Celtic were scheduled to arrive back from Slovenia in the early hours of Sunday, July 10, and needed to be in Gibraltar the following day. Rodgers saw little need for the extra flight and instead triggered a contingency plan that would see the entire party travel direct from Maribor to the British territory in southern Spain via plane and coach.

It led to some upheaval and extra work for Celtic's travel staff but for Rodgers, it was worth the hassle. After an extra night at the Habakuk Hotel, the Celtic squad checked in at Maribor airport the following afternoon for a flight to Malaga.

They were joined in the departure lounge by regiments of the Slovenian army and players again huddled around their laptops and tablets, this time to watch Andy Murray's Wimbledon final. The Celtic party cheered as the Scot proved too strong for Milos Raonic.

It was a historic second SW19 victory for Murray, someone who, like Rodgers, placed great importance on los detallitos.

SHOCK AND AWE

L EE CASCIARO stood at the bottom of a concrete stairwell in the bowels of Lincoln Red Imps' modest Victoria Stadium. Light blue Adidas football boots were hanging limply from his right hand. Beads of sweat dripped from his forehead.

The Gibraltarian, a military policeman, had just scored the winning goal in one of the biggest one-off upsets in modern European football history. It was the greatest moment of his career and he was trying manfully to express his emotions.

Journalists jostled for interview space as Casciaro spoke, while simultaneously accepting the praise of friends, family and strangers. He was still talking everyone through the goal of his life as the Celtic squad walked past, one by one. Heads bowed, they appeared stunned at what had just happened.

This wasn't the start Brendan Rodgers expected. After a successful pre-season tour in Slovenia, the opening

Champions League qualifier with the Red Imps appeared to be a simple introduction to competitive football for the new Celtic manager and his squad.

A part-time team from Gibraltar? What could go wrong? Celtic supporters viewed it as a glorified pre-season friendly, a chance for Leigh Griffiths and Moussa Dembele to get off the mark for the season. It was only a case of how many they would score. What transpired was one of the most incredible and infamous games in Celtic's history.

The club has a rich European background but included in that are some notable upsets. Artmedia Bratislava and Neuchatel Xamax are two relatively obscure European clubs, but the mere mention of their names can send Celtic supporters into cold sweats. By 9.35pm on July 12, 2016, Lincoln Red Imps were added to that list after a surreal evening of Champions League football.

As settings go, the Victoria Stadium is unique in Europe. The tiny stadium sits in the shadow of the Rock of Gibraltar, where Barbary macaques roam free. Behind one goal, a wire fence separates the edge of the basic complex and the Gibraltar airport runway, which doubles as the only road into the territory.

Roaring RAF jets and budget airlines took off as Celtic went through their warm-up just 100 yards away, but in the stifling summer heat, staying cool was the Scottish champions' biggest problem. While clearly technically superior to the Red Imps, Celtic never got to grips with the climate or sticky, outdated artificial surface. From the outset, nothing went to plan.

Celtic struggled to open up the part-timers and when Casciaro escaped Efe Ambrose to send a bouncing shot past Craig Gordon for the opening goal early in the second half, belief surged through the Red Imps. Celtic hit the woodwork a couple of times but the minnows held on. The full-time whistle sparked scenes of jubilation in the packed stand housing local fans. This was their moment.

Rodgers maintained a calm exterior but knew this result would reverberate around Europe. A part-time team from Gibraltar had beaten Celtic. With hardly any other top-level competitive football that night, this was big news, from Scotland to the States.

"Miracles do happen," beamed Red Imps captain Roy Chipolina. In England, sports editors took the rare decision to lead their back-page coverage with a game involving a Scottish team and one of the most embarrassing results in Celtic's history. At the same time, network radio stations frantically searched for the telephone numbers of journalists who had witnessed it all.

It became known as the 'Shock of Gibraltar' but if the Celtic manager felt embarrassed, he didn't show it. Rodgers could have hammered his players with deserved criticism after a lethargic, lifeless performance but instead stressed he had no doubt Celtic would overturn the defeat in the second leg in Glasgow the following week.

"There is obvious disappointment," Rodgers said. "There is no embarrassment. It was a tough game in tough conditions. We didn't take our chances, they took their chance. I'm not really shocked. I've been around the game long enough. I know these results can happen. There is no panic. We stay calm."

The fall-out from the Shock of Gibraltar continued until the start of the second leg. Casciaro enjoyed his 15 minutes of fame as interview requests continued to pour in. "Hopefully we can finish them off in Glasgow," he said tentatively, but there was a never a genuine feeling that the first game would prove fatal for Celtic.

Inspired by a stellar performance from winger Patrick Roberts, who was starting the second part of an 18-month loan from Manchester City, the return tie was a routine 3-0 win for Rodgers' side. The score could easily have reached double figures but goals from Mikael Lustig, Griffiths and Roberts sufficed. Celtic had survived their Gibraltar scare and were now off and running in the Champions League.

Rodgers shook hands with every Red Imps player at full-time. They had given his team a real fright and returned home with their reputation enhanced. The Celtic manager and his squad moved on to tougher tests: the first an arduous trip to Kazakhstan to face Astana in the third qualifying round.

Rodgers joked at Celtic's luck when the opposition was confirmed: "Apart from the six-hour flight, five-hour time difference and the 35 degree heat on a dry plastic pitch, it's not a bad trip." Behind the scenes, it was time to get serious.

With the away leg first in Kazakhstan, preparation was always going to be crucial for the Scottish champions. Rodgers sought advice and created a plan to ensure his players were fresh and ready to play at their peak at the end of an energy-sapping flight.

The club spared no expense by hiring a luxury jet, once used by Madonna, for the journey to Astana, an isolated, space-age city in the middle of the Kazakh Steppe. But this was also an occasion when Glen Driscoll and his sports science team came into their element for Celtic.

Following discussions with Rodgers, they took the decision to keep the squad on Scottish time. This was surprising but the Celtic medical staff felt that any attempt to adjust their body clocks would have been futile, given they only had one full day in Astana before the game.

This meant players eating their evening meal at 2am local time and going to bed a few hours later, in the middle of the night. Long lie-ins were actively encouraged in the morning. "It feels a bit strange but it's the right thing to do," said goalkeeper Craig Gordon.

That wasn't the only surreal aspect of Celtic's pre-match preparations. The regulation UEFA press conference was gate-crashed by the Kazakh Liverpool Supporters' Club, with many travelling hundreds of miles across a vast country just to catch a glimpse of Rodgers and thank him for his work at Anfield. "Brendan, You'll Never Walk Alone" shouted one emotional Liverpool fanatic as the Celtic manager happily posed for photos.

Rodgers was smiling again in the same interview room 24 hours later, after his depleted team had secured a valuable 1-1 away draw on an artificial surface that could have doubled as an ice rink. Given how much Celtic had to contend with, this was a significant step forward for Rodgers and his players.

They earned the draw the hard way. A defensive crisis had deepened 72 hours before the game when Erik Sviatchenko was ruled out with a thigh injury. The Dane was the club's first-choice centre-half and his absence left his manager with a shortage of options in a pivotal area of the pitch.

Already without Dedryck Boyata and Jozo Simunovic through injury, Rodgers had added Kolo Toure to his squad by then but the experienced Ivorian had barely trained with his team-mates and wasn't deemed fit enough to feature.

Ambrose, an experienced yet erratic central defender, had been at the centre of several European calamities for Celtic in previous years and evidently did not have a long-term future under the new manager. Yet he was now the senior man on the trip and Eoghan O'Connell, at just 20, teamed up with the Nigerian in a makeshift partnership.

Celtic rode their luck for a spell after falling behind to Yuri Logvinenko's first-half header. Yet for the most part, Ambrose and O'Connell performed admirably. There was the odd scare but the young Irishman, in particular, delivered a display full of poise and composure. Rodgers gave him clear, simple instructions and he followed them to the letter.

In attack, Roberts again proved massively influential as his persistence and skill set up Griffiths for a clinical late equaliser. From the moment the ball was nudged into his path on the corner of the box, a goal was inevitable. The explosive finish was Griffiths at his predatory best.

When the striker swept in a penalty in the first half of the second leg in Glasgow, Celtic looked in good shape, despite an early hamstring injury forcing Roberts off. Yet Agim Ibraimi's instinctive lob over Gordon in the second half meant the Kazakh club were just one goal away from progressing, as the game entered its closing stages.

During the pre-season trip to Slovenia, Rodgers had constantly spoken to his players about the need to be mentally and physically fit in order to succeed at this elite level. Astana sensed Celtic's uncertainty but Rodgers' players found a way, just like he'd asked them to.

Substitute Dembele linked with Griffiths to win a last-minute penalty and showed composure beyond his 20 years to convert it. As the Frenchman's shot nestled in the net, Celtic Park erupted in an awesome spectacle of noise and colour. They were through. Astana, an awkward opponent, had been eliminated.

It later transpired that the winning goal had been the first penalty of Dembele's senior career. "The manager sent me on and told me it would be a good time to get my first Celtic goal," he said. "I felt a little bit of pressure with the penalty but as a striker, you have to score."

The Astana match was Rodgers' first experience of a dramatic, intense European night at Celtic Park. This was the high he craved when he took the job and he savoured the celebrations at full-time, while also pleading with the fans to show less anxiety at testing moments.

"It was a wonderful atmosphere, brilliant support and they helped push us over the line," he said. "But they need to show a bit of patience as well. I'm a Celtic supporter myself, I know what they want, I know how desperately they want it, but they put the players on edge at times."

To gently reprimand the fans in public so early in his Celtic reign was a brave move by Rodgers but there were very few grumbles in response. Instead, there was a growing feeling that Celtic were on the verge of something special under the new manager.

Rodgers was now just one step away from the Champions League. The Shock of Gibraltar already felt like a lifetime ago.

NEVER DIE WONDERING

ALONA BARKAT is the First Lady of Israeli football. Driven and ambitious, the glamorous businesswoman had a clear vision for Hapoel Be'er Sheva's long-term future when she bought the club for around £1.2million in 2007.

Be'er Sheva were languishing in Israel's lower leagues at that point but Barkat had a masterplan that would eventually lead this small, unfashionable desert outfit all the way to the Champions League qualifiers. By August 2016, only Celtic and Brendan Rodgers stood between her and what once felt like the impossible dream of reaching the group stages.

The general reaction among Celtic players and supporters when they drew Be'er Sheva in the Champions League play-off was: Who? This was the Israeli's club debut in the competition after winning their first title in 40 years. Celtic were overwhelming favourites to progress.

It was a dangerous scenario. Rodgers did his homework

on Celtic's opponents and warned that Be'er Sheva should not be underestimated. This was a talented team of substance and a club of promise, underpinned by Barkat's business nous and the intelligence of manager Barak Bakhar.

A serious, squat figure, the Be'er Sheva coach had masterminded the 2015/16 title win and led the club to this play-off against Celtic, eliminating Champions League regulars Olympiakos on the way. This 1-0 aggregate win for the Israelis was a major surprise and led to the Greek club sacking manager Victor Sanchez after just 47 days in charge.

Be'er Sheva's co-efficient rating was almost non-existent but they represented a difficult test for Rodgers' men, especially as the second leg was away from home in the suffocating heat of the Israeli summer.

With this in mind, it was widely accepted that the first game would be pivotal. Celtic were determined to take a comfortable lead into the return match but were again destined to do things the hard way on another frenetic, dramatic night of European football.

The key moment of the August 17 first leg arrived at around 8.50pm, just 12 minutes into the second half on a balmy Glasgow evening. Maor Melikson's first-time shot exploded past Craig Gordon and Celtic Park instantly fell silent, barring the screams of a few hundred Be'er Sheva supporters penned in at a corner of the Lisbon Lions stand.

Rodgers turned away from the pitch and began to think. It wasn't an easy thing to do. There was pandemonium all around him as home supporters reacted to the Be'er Sheva goal with a mixture of fury and disbelief.

Having cruised to a 3-0 half-time lead against the Israeli

side, Celtic had now conceded two away goals within two minutes. They were fighting for their Champions League future. Out of nowhere, Be'er Sheva had grabbed control of the tie.

Rodgers had prepared for these moments and knew he had to remain calm. He was faced with a choice: protect Celtic's now slender lead and at least head to Israel with a win, or go for broke and keep attacking.

Earlier that night, the Green Brigade section of the Celtic support had urged Rodgers to 'Go All In' with a poker-themed pre-match display. Yet the man in the home dug-out didn't need convincing that attack was the best form of defence at that decisive moment.

"I'll never die wondering," said Rodgers, after late goals from substitute Moussa Dembele and captain Scott Brown gave Celtic a priceless 5-2 win.

"You are either a coach who waits or creates. I come from the creative side. I always think, whether it is in life or football, if you rely on yourself, then you can be happy. Because at least if you fail, you fail on your terms. So that's by creating, right? If I wait, I'm reliant on someone else. In life, you only rely on yourself, the team and the people around you."

Patience from the stands was also needed to dig Celtic out of the situation against Be'er Sheva. After the Astana victory, Rodgers hadn't been slow to remind the supporters of the part they would play in a successful Champions League qualifying campaign.

In the minutes following Be'er Sheva's second goal, there was audible frustration but noticeably less panic than in the previous round against the Kazakhs. This was crucial as the Celtic players didn't need reminding that they were on the verge of messing up. "At 3-2, I thought,

'This is Malmo all over again,'" said Leigh Griffiths, who had scored twice in a dynamic first-half display. He wasn't the only one inside Celtic Park experiencing that sense of dread.

The Swedish club's name cropped up regularly during Celtic's Champions League qualifiers, due to a collapse from Ronny Deila's side in the play-off 12 months earlier. Leading 2-0 and 3-1 in the first leg, they contrived to go out 4-3 on aggregate.

The pain of that defeat in southern Sweden, and the 2014 failure against Maribor, was still raw for Celtic players and supporters. Be'er Sheva's two-goal burst understandably led to fears of a similar outcome, but Rodgers was in control.

"The manager showed he has balls," was Griffiths' unique post-match analysis live on BT Sport.

That colourful language led to howls of laughter from host Gary Lineker and analyst, Scotland manager Gordon Strachan, yet Griffiths was making a valid, serious point.

In introducing Nir Bitton to regain control of the midfield, and Dembele to pose Be'er Sheva fresh problems in attack, Rodgers showed he had the bravery and belief in his judgement to make big decisions under huge pressure.

"At 3-2 against Be'er Sheva, I thought, 'We are really dominant in the game here but a little inexperience in defence has cost us. That has given them a bit of life, a bit of oxygen. But we've enough quality on the pitch to hurt them'. So we then go a little more offensive and it puts us on the front foot again," said Rodgers.

Celtic's thrilling first-leg finale did more than turn the tie back in their favour, it ultimately sealed a place in the group stages. Brown's precise volley, his side's fifth of a pulsating match, gave Rodgers' men a three-goal advantage to take to Israel for the second leg. They needed it on a nerve-shredding night in Israel.

The Celtic manager described the return game against Be'er Sheva as "the longest 90 minutes of my coaching career". The Scottish champions lost 2-0 in the sweltering heat of the Negev but did just enough to progress.

"Trust yourselves," Rodgers told his players before they took to the Turner Stadium pitch, but it took two changes of formation before they looked remotely comfortable in a game worth an estimated £30million to the club. Pounds and prestige were at stake.

Be'er Sheva had a formidable home record and went straight for the jugular. Gordon saved Maharan Radi's penalty in 15 minutes after a rash Saidy Janko tackle but that only delayed the breakthrough. Ben Sahar headed the Israelis into the lead before half-time and within three minutes of the restart, Be'er Sheva added a second. Again, Celtic's inexperienced right-back Janko was at fault when he ran into Gordon, who spilled the ball for Ovidiu Hoban to convert.

Celtic were now within one goal of being knocked out at the Champions League play-off stage for a third successive season. Rodgers was under major pressure. His players appeared crippled by nerves. The manager's initial team selection and tactics hadn't worked but again, he didn't panic.

A major criticism of Deila in those defining Champions League qualifiers had been an inability to adapt and manage the flow of the game. Against Malmo especially, he had seemed unwilling or unable to move from his formation of choice and make changes to influence the outcome. The Norwegian paid the ultimate price for an indecisive streak. In the Be'er Sheva away match, Rodgers started with a 4-3-3 formation and then moved to a midfield diamond. But in the second half, the Celtic boss changed his system for a second time, sending on Erik Sviatchenko as a third central defender beside Mikael Lustig and Kolo Toure. Finally, Celtic looked comfortable and the closing stages were surprisingly stress-free as the Israelis ran out of ideas.

Sviatchenko carried a handwritten note on to the pitch when he entered, passing it to captain Brown. "What did the note say? Danger!" said Rodgers afterwards. "Seriously, it was just to make sure they understood the shape from what we were doing.

"If you leave the message with a player, sometimes it doesn't get on quick enough. Scotty's a great communicator, so Erik gave it to him and he could see the shape of the team and what personnel had to go to what positions and what we were trying to achieve. You then rip it up quickly and go.

"I've used these notes in the past. You have to be short, sharp and concise with your information. However you get it on there, whether it is written or verbal, you need to get the message through. I thought we then found calmness."

Yet Celtic were still walking a tightrope and the final whistle from referee Bas Nijhuis triggered a mixture of relief and jubilation. Even Rodgers, normally reserved in the aftermath of significant wins, let himself go for once. Wide-eyed and elated, he walked towards the Celtic supporters and pumped the Celtic badge on his chest as he embraced his exhausted players.

The celebrations continued long into the night at the local Leonardo Hotel as Celtic staff and players savoured the achievement. For Rodgers, it was mission accomplished. Within weeks of taking over, he had led the club back to the Champions League. For the players, who suffered pain and embarrassment against Maribor and Malmo, it was redemption.

"It was always going to be about resilience and persistence," Rodgers said, after finally breaking away from the celebrations. "It was an amazing effort from the players on the back of everything they have been through before. I'm immensely proud and it's an incredible moment for the supporters. Being back among Europe's elite is where this club belongs."

Rodgers would have preferred to qualify in a more convincing manner against Be'er Sheva, but with £30million and the prestige of the tournament at stake, getting to the group stages was all that really mattered for Celtic. Not that it prevented Roy Keane, the club's outspoken former midfielder, criticising the manager and his players for their celebrations in Israel.

"They were poor, they scraped through," said the Irishman on ITV. "The whole mindset has to change. Don't accept, especially away from home, being the whipping boys of Europe. It's Celtic, a huge club.

"When they qualified for the group, the celebrations, for me, were way over the top. I actually thought they'd won the competition. People were hugging each other, the manager, the coaches, the players. It's not Altrincham, it's Celtic."

Rodgers was made aware of this outburst but recalled the Republic of Ireland assistant manager's own reaction when his country made it to the Euro 2016 finals via a play-off.

"When Ireland qualified for the Euros I think that

was an achievement," said Rodgers, pointedly. "I don't think there were too many of the staff not smiling or hugging.

"We went through six real tough qualification games. Until you actually come through it, until you actually experience the emotion and what it means to people... we have to fight to get there. The players have every right to celebrate, out of relief, out of ambition.

"It's very important that the players can celebrate a milestone. If you're always running the race, you never get the feeling of going over the finish line. It was our first goal of the season and we achieved it. It meant a lot to the club. It meant a lot to the players."

The importance of Celtic's qualification only heightened after the Champions League group stage draw was made. The Scottish club were the last team picked out by Roberto Carlos and their fate had already been sealed. Celtic were in Group C with Barcelona, Manchester City and Borussia Monchengladbach.

In terms of glamour, Celtic couldn't have asked for any more. In terms of difficulty, Rodgers and his players knew that nobody gave them a prayer. Within minutes of the draw, bookmakers offered odds on Celtic failing to pick up a single point in the group.

Yet the sneering made no difference to Rodgers. "We have to do our best," he said. "I don't think it's right to go into it and just be the also-ran. Everyone knows it's going to be extremely tough, but we have got to embrace this challenge."

Embrace it Celtic did, and nobody more so than Rodgers. After the disappointing end to his Liverpool reign less than a year earlier, the Northern Irishman was rebuilding his reputation and operating at the elite level of the Champions League again. His decision to take the Celtic job had already been vindicated.

Invincible

LOCAL KNOWLEDGE

"WHAT'S Gary Bollan up to these days?" Brendan Rodgers interrupts a Sunday newspaper press conference with a question of his own on his first day as Celtic manager.

After being informed that the former Dundee United and Rangers defender is now managing Forfar Athletic in Scotland's League Two, Rodgers explains his unexpected interest. "I played for Northern Ireland under-16s against Scotland and Gary was the captain," he says.

This kind of anecdote becomes a regular occurrence when spending any time in Rodgers' company. The Celtic manager possesses a photographic memory when it comes to football and his career experiences. Names, faces, he remembers it all.

A few weeks later, he met up with Dunfermline manager Allan Johnston at an SPFL launch event at Falkirk's Kelpies attraction. "He would probably never remember it, but I recall being at Manchester United as a young player when Allan was there," said Rodgers. "We were 13... we both look a lot different now."

Later in the season, Duncan Shearer, a member of the Inverness Caledonian Thistle backroom staff, would relay his shock that the Celtic manager, without any prompting, recalled his presence alongside Shearer on a Largs coaching course some 20 years earlier.

This familiarity helped Rodgers adjust to the Scottish game. This had been a problem for his predecessor Ronny Deila. The Norwegian didn't know the histories and personalities of clubs and managers he encountered on a weekly basis and never quite seemed to get to grips with it all. Deila rarely name-checked or spoke at length about opposition players or coaches, but from day one, Rodgers seemed comfortable in his surroundings and full of respect for his peers.

Premiership rivals Robbie Neilson, Derek McInnes, Mark McGhee, Tommy Wright and Jim McIntyre were all mentioned on the day he was unveiled at Celtic Park. Mark Warburton, the Rangers manager until departing in February, had worked in Watford's academy when Rodgers was manager at Vicarage Road.

Others, like Hearts' Neilson, who would leave for MK Dons in December, had been to visit Rodgers during his time at Liverpool and Swansea, while more had become friends or acquaintances after meeting on the football circuit.

"There are good guys up here," said Rodgers. "I looked through all the managers working in Scotland because I was interested to know. It's a totally different world for me but it was nice to see familiar names."

Rodgers' relationship with his fellow managers was generally positive, barring a disagreement with McGhee after a 4-3 win over Motherwell at Fir Park in December. A pre-match issue over Celtic using the goal area for their warm-up spilled over after the game, with Rodgers' assistant Chris Davies clashing with McGhee. The Motherwell manager claimed his behaviour "wasn't Celtic quality" but Rodgers countered that by stating McGhee's own conduct wasn't "befitting of the assistant manager of Scotland and manager of Motherwell".

That was a rare glimpse of Rodgers' steely side, but it was the only incident of its type during the course of the season. In general, the Celtic manager made a real effort to get along with his contemporaries and offer support and advice to the younger generation whenever they needed it.

"Brendan coming to Celtic has given the Scottish game a lift," said Dundee manager Paul Hartley in March. "He's managed at the top level and it's good to test yourself against him. But he's also someone you can pick the phone up and talk to. When we first met, he gave me his number straight away."

Just a month later, Hartley was out of work, having lost his job at Dens Park. One of the first people on the phone to him was Rodgers. He immediately extended an invitation to the former Celtic player to spend a day at Lennoxtown, which Hartley accepted in early May. "Brendan was different class with me," he said.

Rodgers' door was always open. Jack Ross, St Mirren's progressive young coach, earned huge praise from his opposite number after Celtic's 4-1 Scottish Cup win over the Paisley club. The game was a lot tighter than the scoreline suggested and Rodgers told Ross to visit Lennoxtown whenever he wanted. "Brendan has been great to me personally," said Ross. "I was also at Celtic with Alloa earlier in the season and I've really enjoyed our conversations."

Rodgers' awareness of the Scottish game even extended to the fringe and young players he inherited at Celtic. He had done his homework on every single member of the squad but listening to him, without any prompting, recall his first sighting of Nadir Ciftci as a kid at Portsmouth six years earlier and offer in-depth thoughts on how the striker's career had evolved since then was as unexpected as it was impressive.

The new Celtic manager embraced Scottish football and never gave the impression that he treated it as a step down from the English game. "I've thought of going to The Emirates on a Tuesday or Wednesday night or going to Inverness, but it's football," he said, when asked about the lack of glitz in Scotland's Premiership. "I'm from a council estate in Northern Ireland so I'm not a snob.

"Football is football. You represent the team and you go anywhere with them, whether it's up the road or in Europe. It's different but I'm looking forward to it. There are more glamorous surroundings to go and work in but I have a real passion to do well here."

Before he had even accepted the Celtic job, Rodgers began studying footage of the 2015/16 season to gain an understanding of the squad he would inherit. By the time he officially took over, he had studied every single goal scored and conceded in the previous campaign.

Davies was also involved in this painstaking process, watching dozens of DVDs during late May and early June. This research allowed the new management team to gain an idea of what awaited them when the squad arrived back for pre-season training and, specifically, which areas they urgently needed to improve.

"It's a real thorough process," said Davies at his own unveiling inside Celtic Park's Walfrid restaurant. "That's how we work and we're just looking to understand the landscape of where the club is at and where the players are at.

"That's important to us because we weren't in there last season and it means we can objectively look at things without emotion. Watching it all gives us an idea. We've seen enough footage so far to tell us what we need to know about the team. It's important to understand that because it can help you to plan forward."

This research didn't just extend to the Celtic squad. Rodgers has a strict method of preparing for opponents and didn't allow his staff to deviate from this regardless of the importance of the game and the status of the opposition.

In Graz, during Celtic's pre-season campaign, one local journalist appeared in complete shock when the Celtic manager was able to reel off stats and tactical information about the Austrian club.

This was a low-key friendly but Rodgers had committed to preparing for it like it was a Champions League qualifier. Footage of Sturm Graz's previous games was accessed as the Celtic backroom staff studied it to gain any possible advantage.

"The preparation is always exactly the same, every game is studied to the umpteenth degree," said Rodgers ahead of a January Scottish Cup tie with part-time Albion Rovers.

"The minute you don't prepare is when you have an issue, you become loose and soft. That's when you suffer. The minute we knew Albion were our next opponents we afforded them the same respect as Barcelona, Manchester

City and Borussia Monchengladbach. We've looked at all the details this week.

"I know Albion are seventh in League One. They're well organised, play a 4-2-3-1, they're quite direct and play off a second ball quite a lot. This is another game we must ensure we approach with the same level of concentration as the others we've played this season. No matter the league in which they play, we must concentrate."

'We'll treat Albion Rovers like Barcelona' made for a great headline but Rodgers wasn't just offering nice soundbites. He didn't tolerate standards dropping when it came to preparing for the opposition. The analysis template he favoured had been in use from his early managerial days. By the time he arrived at Celtic, it had been updated and improved countless times.

This high level of preparation, allied to Celtic's existing quality and improved fitness under Rodgers, was a promising combination. The Scottish season kicked off on August 7 and the reigning champions were already in a strong place by that point. The first four Premiership games would be against Hearts, St Johnstone, Aberdeen and Rangers, and the new Celtic manager was determined to make an emphatic early statement on the domestic scene.

SCOTT SINCLAIR

THE LOGICAL ONE

Oh Scotty Sinclair, oh he is so wonderful,
When he scores a goal, oh it's beautiful, magical.
When he runs down the wing he's as fast as lightning,
It's frightening... and he makes the Bhoys sing

ROGER HODGSON was in Los Angeles, sitting at a Wurlitzer electric piano. It was during a 1978 tour and the Supertramp frontman was experimenting with a new chord progression. Suddenly a melody hit him. By the end of that session, Hodgson had the basic structure of what would become *The Logical Song*, his band's biggest hit in both Britain and America.

Almost four decades later, that same tune written by Hodgson in the Californian sunshine could be heard in football stadiums up and down Scotland. Inspired by Scooter's dance version, Celtic supporters borrowed the melody and altered its lyrics to pay tribute to Scott Sinclair.

The song choice was fitting. For Brendan Rodgers, the English winger was always the logical signing of the summer transfer window. From the moment the new manager took over at Celtic, Sinclair topped a list of targets compiled with quality, not quantity, in mind.

Rodgers knew exactly what he was getting when he urged the club's board to sanction a fee in excess of £3million to Aston Villa for the fleet-footed, daring winger. It took five bids to finally get him but just one appearance and one goal for the Celtic fans to take Sinclair to their hearts. The terrace anthem would arrive soon after.

Sometimes players fit like a glove at certain clubs. Sinclair and Celtic are a prime example of that rare perfect match. He scored the winner soon after coming on as a substitute on his debut against Hearts on August 7. Sinclair raced the full length of the park as Celtic broke at speed from a corner and was in the perfect place to convert Leigh Griffiths' low cross.

Sinclair quickly became a pivotal figure for Celtic and was a huge influence on the team's success. Full of pace and purpose, and capable of matching hard work with guile, he set the tone for Rodgers' team in an attacking sense. When Celtic returned to Tynecastle on April 2 to wrap up the title with a 5-0 win, Sinclair finished what he had started with a clinical hat-trick.

Given his instant impact at Celtic, it seems surprising that no English clubs fought Rodgers for Sinclair's services during the summer. His transfer from Villa was protracted but only because the newly-relegated club were determined to squeeze every penny out of the Scottish champions. Yet, in the crazy world of English football's inflated fees, Celtic got themselves a bargain.

The main reason for this is that the winger had been written off by many in England. The former Swansea and Manchester City attacker was wrongly viewed as just another promising player who had failed to fulfil his potential. Rodgers knew better and was convinced Sinclair could recapture the form he had shown during their successful time together at Swansea.

A former Chelsea youth player, he had blossomed in Wales as a vital cog in Rodgers' free-flowing Swansea team. Sinclair's selection for Team GB at the 2012 London Olympics only enhanced his reputation. England recognition seemed inevitable, but joining City that summer was the wrong turn in a career that had been on an upwards trajectory until that point.

City manager Roberto Mancini came in with an £8million offer on the last day of the 2012 summer transfer window and it was too good an opportunity for Sinclair and Swansea to turn down. Yet, after a promising start, he fell out of favour and left City having made just two Premier League starts. It was a financially lucrative spell for Sinclair but stalled his progression as a footballer and led to a difficult period in his life.

"I was going through a stage at City where I was coming home every day and I was angry and snappy," said Sinclair. "Getting to the weekend, not being in the squad and training, sometimes by myself, that was the hardest time. It went on for months and months.

"All my family noticed I wasn't myself, but people who look from the outside say, 'Ah, you're fine because you've had the contract'. For me football means more than just that.

"People will always say, 'Well why did you go to City then?' but at that time it was a great opportunity and when you want to become the best you can be you want to be playing with the best."

Loan moves at West Brom and Aston Villa followed, before a permanent transfer to the Midlands club. Playing in a struggling side at Villa Park, he was unable to reach the heights of his Swansea days. Deep down, Sinclair was still haunted by his stifling City experience. Then Rodgers offered him a way out at Celtic, a chance to enjoy life as a footballer once more.

"My main aim when I joined Celtic was to be happy again," he said. "That stage of my career at Villa was very tough, but you need to go through periods like that.

"What happened then made me stronger as a person. It made me even hungrier and made me want to play regularly again. I came to Celtic to do that and from the first day, I never looked back. I've been at a lot of clubs but I feel I have found a home here."

Rodgers knew how to press Sinclair's buttons, having first encountered him at Chelsea as a 16-year-old. The Stamford Bridge club plucked him from Bristol Rovers and he was converted from a tricky centre-forward into an effective left-sided attacker. When Rodgers took over at Swansea in 2010, he was a priority signing. Sinclair scored 27 goals including a hat-trick in the play-off final as Swansea won promotion to the Premier League.

Six years after signing Sinclair for the first time, Rodgers set about reviving his career at Celtic. It was a case of the right club at the right time for both men. Rodgers believed in his protégé and gave him the confidence to express himself and play with a freedom that had been lost from his game.

"Scott has always been about enjoying his football," said Rodgers in early August, after finally getting his man following a two-month pursuit. "The last four years have been really difficult for him.

"I brought him to Swansea, where he was outstanding. That got him a move to Manchester City but from there, really his career stalled. No one has really seen the best of him and they probably forgot about his qualities. But this was a guy who scored a hat-trick in a play-off final under big pressure in front of 90,000. He has a big talent.

"Scotty is physically strong, robust and loves the big occasion. He knows he had to get his career going again. At Aston Villa he always seemed to play full-back. I always felt with Scotty you had to get him 50 metres higher up the pitch to help teams and hopefully he can recreate that here at Celtic."

Rodgers' vision for Sinclair at Celtic didn't take long to crystallise on the pitch. Following his debut winner against Hearts, the goals kept coming. He became the first Celtic player to score in his first six league matches for the club since Jimmy McGrory in the 1930s. Yet his influence wasn't just limited to putting the ball in the net.

Sinclair quickly developed a dynamic partnership with Kieran Tierney on Celtic's left flank but was at his most effective drifting infield to knit the play together, and luring markers out of position to create gaps for others to exploit. His goal threat was a major asset for Celtic and his touch, pace, movement and awareness were consistently on a different level to anyone else in the Scottish game.

There was also his wider influence on the squad. Sinclair had been there and done it in England, having operated at a high level and experienced life at a modern superclub in City. As a sounding board for coveted young players like Moussa Dembele and Tierney, his presence and advice was invaluable. He was careful not to interfere too much but viewed his own career as proof that the grass isn't always greener elsewhere.

"I have spoken to Moussa about decisions," said Sinclair. "When you look down in England, there are not many players of a young age playing with the top three clubs, week in and week out. If Moussa is happy here, then you cannot get anything better than that. At the back of his head, he will still have the dream to play for a Barcelona or a Real Madrid or whatever, but it is all about timing."

Sinclair led by example for Rodgers, on and off the pitch. He has millions in the bank and a celebrity girlfriend in Coronation Street's Helen Flanagan, while his blonde Mohawk hairstyle is instantly recognisable. Yet he is as grounded a footballer as you will find in the British game. Modest and polite to a fault, he was the ideal pro for Rodgers, with the maturity to match his undoubted ability.

The winger's derby winner against Rangers at Ibrox on New Year's Eve was his 12th goal of the season and came after he'd spent four weeks in November and December on the sidelines with a hamstring injury. On his return, his ability to adapt to a more central role when Dembele and Leigh Griffiths were out injured ensured Celtic retained a cutting edge. By the end of the season, Sinclair had claimed 25 goals and 11 assists, and scooped every Player of the Year award available, including one from his Celtic team-mates.

Rodgers' other main summer signing, Dembele, captured more headlines and attention than Sinclair but arguably no Celtic player contributed more than the English winger over the course of the season. Rodgers' unshakable belief and insistence on the long summer pursuit of Sinclair proved to be a masterstroke. Sinclair's performances were of such a high standard that there were those inside Celtic Park who breathed an enormous sigh of relief when the January transfer window passed without any serious bids from England.

The focus during the winter window was all on Dembele's future and Chelsea's public pursuit of Craig Gordon. Yet Sinclair was a player with the quality and athleticism to play at a high level in the Premier League. However, no manager knew how to harness his talent quite like Rodgers.

Sinclair was an impressive summer transfer coup for Celtic as the new manager opted to largely target tried and trusted players from his previous clubs for key positions. With the key Champions League qualifiers coming so early in the season, Rodgers couldn't afford to gamble with his recruitment.

In this sense, Kolo Toure was another influential signing. The Ivorian was 35 by the time he completed his move to Celtic in late July but Rodgers, having worked with the defender at Liverpool, felt his experience and personality would be crucial in the early months of the season.

Like Sinclair, Toure represented a major outlay in wages for Celtic, in Scottish terms, but they got an immediate return for their investment. With lengthy injuries to central defenders Jozo Simunovic and Dedryck Boyata, Rodgers needed an experienced leader in that crucial area in the short term and Toure provided those qualities, especially against Hapoel Be'er Sheva in the play-off.

As the season progressed and players returned from injury, Toure's appearances became rare. He was exposed in a Champions League game with Borussia

Monchengladbach and a nagging groin injury hindered his involvement on the pitch around the turn of the year. By the time he had recovered, Simunovic and Boyata were established alongside Erik Sviatchenko. Yet, in the background Rodgers deemed Toure's influence to be invaluable for a young Celtic squad.

"I brought Kolo here for a number of reasons," said Rodgers. "One of them was to help us get through to the Champions League. His mentality, and the experience of what it takes to get there, was going to be important. There are other reasons, like his influence in the changing room. Scott Brown is a wonderful leader but it's nice for him to have someone like Kolo behind him with his big-game experience."

As the season progressed, Toure worked closely in training with Celtic's academy players. Teenage striker Jack Aitchison revealed the well-travelled defender was constantly imparting his wisdom to him, while Boyata viewed Toure as an inspiration during his battle to regain a first-team spot.

"Kolo is a very good person, a very important person in my life," said the Belgian defender. "When I was down he was always telling me 'Don't worry, you've just got to wait for your chance, when it comes just take it'. So that was what I did."

Dorus de Vries was the third player signed by Rodgers in the summer window who had previously worked under the Celtic manager. The experienced Dutch goalkeeper arrived from Nottingham Forest in mid-August and had ousted Craig Gordon within two weeks. Injury and De Vries' patchy form would allow the Scotland internationalist to regain his place and he never once looked like giving it up. Cristian Gamboa, an experienced

Costa Rican, was also brought in from West Brom to provide competition in the right-back area. Mikael Lustig remained in possession of that jersey for the season but Gamboa, a quick and able full-back, never let Rodgers down when called upon.

The Celtic manager signed five players in total, with Dembele another inspired capture. Celtic exploited cross-border compensation rules to sign him for a paltry £500,000 from Fulham. A regular scorer in the Championship, the teenager was valued at £8million by the Craven Cottage club. If Dembele had moved elsewhere in England, they would have asked the Professional Football Compensation Committee to set a fee amounting to millions.

Yet Celtic's football development manager John Park, who left in October, was well-versed in FIFA transfer legislation between associations. Joe Ledley had been signed from Cardiff City in 2010 on a similar basis and Celtic knew they would have to pay a minimal training compensation fee for Dembele. In terms of football and finance, it was incredible business. By the time a prolific season was over, the French forward's value had soared to astronomical levels.

Fulham were disappointed to miss out on a bigger fee but Celtic had acted within the rules. The Craven Cottage club evidently didn't hold a grudge and later in the summer handed over £2million for the signing of Stefan Johansen. The Norwegian midfielder, Scotland's Player of the Year in 2014/15, was a relatively high-profile departure from Celtic after contract extension talks ended in stalemate.

Charlie Mulgrew, Celtic's vice-captain, also exited on a free. Rodgers had been eager to retain the versatile Scotland player but after spending the bulk of his career at Celtic, Mulgrew was keen to head south and signed for Blackburn Rovers in the English Championship.

Colin Kazim-Richards, Carlton Cole, Anthony Stokes and Stefan Scepovic were among several other senior players to leave Celtic in the early weeks of Rodgers' reign. The new manager was clear in his desire to trim his squad numbers and ruthless in doing so. As the Sinclair signing demonstrated, quality was all that counted for Rodgers.

HE AIN'T IN MY LEAGUE

MARSEILLE, June 11, 2016. The old port town on France's south coast is gradually coming to life and Joey Barton, dressed in plain light blue shorts and a white t-shirt, is holding court in a city-centre flat doubling as a radio studio.

There as a guest of the UK-based talkSPORT station for a segment of the Euro 2016 tournament, the new Rangers midfielder is offering an opinion on everything and anything in his own inimitable fashion. Surrounded by hi-tech equipment, Barton is joined on the breakfast show by presenter Alan Brazil.

The larger-than-life Scot, a diehard Celtic supporter, is at talkSPORT's French base camp 800 kilometres away in Paris, but effortlessly controls the flow of the conversation, allowing Barton to air his outspoken views.

Back in Scotland, Rangers fans are desperate to hear their box-office signing's thoughts on the season ahead.

Brazil knows his audience and finds a few spare minutes to move away from the Euros and on to the SPFL Premiership.

There are no loaded questions from the talkSPORT host. Instead, he gradually nudges Barton towards the topic of Celtic and the man expected to be his main midfield rival in Scotland: Scott Brown. The results are explosive.

"People keep talking about Joey Barton and Scott Brown," said Barton, sitting perched on the edge of a white recliner chair. "He ain't in my league. He is nowhere near the level I am as a player. He can't get to me. If I play well, Scott Brown doesn't stand a chance. That is not me being blasé. That is me just stating what I believe."

Barton had yet to kick a ball in Scotland and was already targeting the Alpha Male of the nation's football scene, dismissing the Celtic captain's ability and questioning his credentials as a big-time player. The interview went viral within minutes. Social media was in instant meltdown.

Brown was made fully aware of Barton's boasts and incendiary comments later that day. He was given the opportunity to make an immediate public response but politely declined. "I'll do my talking on the pitch," was his private reaction.

Months later, after his Rangers career had ended prematurely amid huge controversy, Barton admitted he was a bit "brash" with his pre-season vows. Others within the Scottish game, some even associated with his own club, felt his trash-talking towards Brown and, subsequently, Celtic manager Brendan Rodgers, had gone too far and was instead bordering on disrespectful.

At that point of the summer, Brown was still the Celtic and Scotland captain and a player of vast experience. He was entering his tenth season at the club, had collected 50 Scotland caps, made more Champions League appearances than any other player in Celtic's history and was about to take his trophy haul as captain into double figures

Brown also wasn't short of team-mates willing to defend him in the weeks following Barton's comments.

"You know Joey Barton has obviously got a mouth on him," was Leigh Griffiths' typically blunt assessment. "How many caps has Joey got? Just the one for England? Broony has 50 for Scotland, he's the captain of his national team, won titles and competed in the Champions League.

"It's up to Barton to say what he wants. But look at Broony's CV. Now look at Joey Barton's CV and everything he's done in his career. Compare the two CVs together... I'm pretty sure I know who I would pick.

"Scott has Champions League experience. He's done it at the very top level of the game, for club and country. If Barton wants to come up here and disrespect him, Broony being Broony will take that in his stride. The first Old Firm game at Celtic Park will be interesting."

The Barton-Brown battle was a fascinating sub-plot to the build-up of the first Celtic-Rangers derby of the season, scheduled for September 10 at Celtic Park. Yet the new Ibrox midfielder wasn't content to merely goad Brown. Rodgers was also in his sights as he continued his noisy arrival into Scottish football.

Barton questioned the tangible success of his managerial career and highlighted the lack of trophies won by the Northern Irishman at Swansea and Liverpool. Up to that point, Rodgers had only won the Championship play-off with the Welsh club.

At Anfield, Rodgers had narrowly failed to get over the

line in a compelling Premier League title race in 2014 and Barton seized on this in another mid-August talkSPORT interview with Brazil. The Rangers midfielder raised doubts over his ability to lead Celtic to the silverware they craved.

"You expect Celtic to improve, they've brought Brendan in and that will be a huge outlay for them," he said. "The only thing you have to quantify that with is — and I'm not trying to stir the pot here, I'm being realistic — Brendan has never won a trophy, he's never won anything.

"He's going to have to do stuff up there he hasn't done before. He's a great manager and a great appointment which will be good for Scottish football but second for Celtic next year is nothing."

If Barton's aim was to crank up the pressure on Celtic, it backfired spectacularly when the two sides met on a sunny September afternoon in Glasgow's East End.

Sky Sports had the live TV rights and gave the fixture a big build-up, billing it as Barton v Brown. For Scottish football, this was box-office stuff.

Hundreds of thousands watched on TV as a crowd of over 58,000 gathered at Celtic Park to see Rodgers' team dismantle their Glasgow rivals and register a season-defining 5-1 victory. For Rangers, it was a humbling defeat and one that ultimately led to the demise of Barton's short-lived Ibrox career.

The Englishman's final act of the game was to nudge two beach balls to the side as he retrieved the match ball from the net following Stuart Armstrong's goal, Celtic's fifth of the afternoon. Given how much he'd had to say for himself over the summer, it was a humiliating experience for Barton. By the end of the rout, he was forced to play as an auxiliary central defender following Philippe Senderos' red card. Clearly short of match fitness after missing the bulk of Rangers' pre-season, Barton had earlier struggled to exert his influence in the crucial midfield area. Brown, in direct contrast, was dominant.

The Celtic captain had already played 10 competitive games by the time Rangers arrived at Celtic Park and looked fitter and stronger than he had in two years.

A slight injury ended Brown's game prematurely on 74 minutes but by then his job was complete. There was only one winner in the Barton v Brown contest as the beaten Rangers midfielder sought his rival out afterwards to offer a handshake and congratulations.

Brown, who had exchanged words with Barton after the second goal of Moussa Dembele's hat-trick, accepted that conciliatory gesture but hadn't forgotten the trash-talking of the summer. He had waited for this moment and made a point of reminding Barton of Celtic's superiority in his post-match interview.

Asked simply 'How was it out there?' Brown said: "Easy. I think the scoreline talks for itself, it was pretty much men versus boys at the end of the day."

Pressed further on what he'd said to Barton after the second goal, he said: "I was just making sure he was alright. Was he? I think so."

It turned out he wasn't. In the days following Celtic's 5-1 victory, Barton stated the Rangers performance was "nowhere near good enough" and then had a verbal clash with team-mate Andy Halliday during training. A subsequent exchange of words with manager Mark Warburton led to him being suspended by Rangers for three weeks.

Barton's Ibrox career was hanging by a thread and he officially severed ties with the club on November 10 after reaching an agreement to end his two-year contract early. That Celtic Park game proved to be his last in a Rangers shirt. He would return to Burnley in the Premier League, before being handed an 18-month ban for breaking FA gambling rules.

Brown was too focused on Celtic to pay undue attention to the circus surrounding Barton. Yet in late October, before the Betfred Cup semi-final win over Rangers, he did open up slightly on the midfielder's fall from grace at Ibrox.

"After the last performance, it's quite amusing," said Brown. "He tried to wind the whole game up and for it to be about him, but top-quality players have come into these games in the past and struggled.

"It's always going to be hard for anyone if they are not going to do the work. He put his team-mates under a lot of pressure while we kept focused, kept on the straight and narrow and just worried about our game, no one else's. I just did my talking on the park rather than in the media."

This theme had been prevalent in the aftermath of Celtic's 5-1 win over Rangers in September, with Rodgers making a point of praising the conduct and discipline of his captain against the noisy backdrop of Barton's goading. Barring a throwaway comment about the Rangers midfielder being a Celtic fan, Brown had said nothing.

"Scott leads the team and is a very respectful guy," said Rodgers. "He bossed the game in the middle of the park. He showed his power, strength and his qualities."

For Rodgers, that first victory over Rangers was another major milestone early in his Celtic reign. He had been able to quickly marry European progress with domestic dominance. Prior to the derby, Celtic had already beaten Hearts and Aberdeen, but Rodgers was aware of the wider significance of the Rangers game.

With that in mind, he made a point of evoking the spirit of Jock Stein and the Lisbon Lions in an emotional, stirring pre-match address to his players as they huddled together inside the home dressing room at Celtic Park.

"Today is the 31st anniversary of Jock Stein's death," said Rodgers afterwards. "This is a guy who created a template here, and I am very proud there is a team today which can play aggressively but fairly, and one which, when things go wrong, can have that mentality to bounce back.

"I spoke about Jock in my team talk. One of his quotes talks about how football is only ever about getting the two points. Back then that's what you got for winning.

"But when I spoke to the players before the game I said: 'For us it's about getting the three points but when you beat one of your rivals it's a wee bit sweeter.' That was the message.

"However, it was primarily about the guy looking down – Jock Stein. He is the man who set the tone for this club, the template. We said that if he is looking down, make sure we do him proud."

Celtic achieved that, and more, against Rangers. Joe Garner's close-range header had made it 2-1 before half-time but Celtic moved up the gears in the second half. Dembele completed his historic, perfect hat-trick and goals from Armstrong and Scott Sinclair sealed a convincing win to send out a defiant title statement.

Yet, during a hectic schedule, there was little time for Celtic to savour the victory over Rangers. There were bigger tests to come for Rodgers and his players as the Champions League kicked off a few days later. Within 48 hours, they were boarding a plane for Barcelona.

A NOU LEVEL

BRENDAN RODGERS always cherished his Barcelona Sundays. He soaked up the 12-hour football fiestas for years as a young coach and those long, lingering days in the sun helped shape his entire vision as a manager.

On September 12, 2016, he found himself back in Catalonia again. Yet this time it was business, not pleasure.

As the Celtic team bus cruised down Avinguda Diagonal and turned right at Avinguda del Doctor Marañón, the imposing Camp Nou appeared in view. It was a familiar sight for Rodgers. He had been there countless times before to worship at the altar of one of world football's iconic cathedrals.

From the moment Rodgers was forced to end his professional playing career at Reading through injury at the age of 20, he vowed to become the best coach he could be. His approach was ambitious, yet simple. To become part of the elite, he had to learn from the elite. Spanish football, and specifically Barcelona, became his inspiration. Rodgers enlisted the help of Julio Delgado, father of the British tennis player Jamie, to learn the language and before long was a regular visitor to Barcelona, studying their methods from top to bottom. These journeys continued even after he became Swansea manager and only travel disruption caused by a volcanic ash cloud prevented him taking up Pep Guardiola's April 2010 invitation to visit for four days. "I was waiting to board my flight when it happened," said Rodgers.

Two years later, Rodgers spent time with the Spain national team at their Euro 2012 training camp, still looking to learn from the then reigning world and European champions. Yet it was Barcelona who always stimulated Rodgers the most, so much so that the passing style of his Swansea side earned them the nickname 'Swanselona' in their early days in the Premier League.

Rodgers shares a birthday with son Anton and on one celebration in his teenage years, he took the impressionable youngster to the Catalan capital for one of those packed, relentless Sunday football marathons.

"I've been coming to Barcelona for a number of years," said Rodgers. "I've always been a great lover of the city and the structure of the club. I admire how the club operates and the values they have.

"Sunday was a great day for me in Barcelona. It's layered on right the way through, with all the kids playing on a Sunday. Then you go into the Mini Estadi and you watch the second team and then onto the main stadium to watch the first team.

"It's a great sporting city and I loved the whole feel of the place. They all played the same, there were individuals, but they played in a structure. It wasn't totally scripted, there was improvisation. I hate mechanical teams, stiff teams that stick to a script. You need improvisation.

"I don't like soloists. If you just have the one player then if God doesn't turn him on in the morning, the whole team suffers. It's that wee mixture of structure and improvisation, and Barcelona have that."

On that birthday trip to Barcelona with his son, the Rodgers boys watched the club's B team, who were then coached by Luis Enrique. Less than 10 years later, he was back in the city to share a touchline at the Camp Nou with the man who had now graduated to become Barca's first-team coach.

Enrique wasn't the only familiar face awaiting him. Rodgers will forever be inextricably linked with the career of Luis Suarez after helping to mould the Uruguayan into arguably the world's best striker during their time together at Liverpool. In the build-up to Celtic's Champions League opener at the Camp Nou, both men spoke of their admiration for each other.

"Luis is the best striker in the world right now," said Rodgers. "He is one of the most beautiful men you can come across. He's a very humble guy who works tirelessly at his profession."

Suarez was similarly full of praise for his old Anfield manager. "If it was not for Brendan, then I know I would not be the same player that you see at Barcelona today," he said. "Such a big part of my education is down to him and his management."

Those were nice words from a world-class footballer, but Rodgers knew that Suarez didn't do sentiment on the pitch.

Neil Lennon, the former Celtic manager, believes one of Barcelona's biggest assets is their ruthless streak. For all their *tiki-taka* passing and mesmerising attacking football, they have also proved to be better than any team at killing the opposition off. "These guys will cut your throat," said Lennon.

Having studied Barcelona closely for the best part of two decades, Rodgers acknowledged that Enrique had more attacking talent and firepower at his disposal than any of the previous managers. The MSN trident of Suarez, Lionel Messi and Neymar was arguably the best frontline ever.

Guardiola had taken the club to a new level during his trophy-laden, four-year spell as manager. He created the modern Barcelona, building on Johan Cruyff's inspirational Total Football template. Guardiola's 2011 team was the benchmark, arguably the best club side in football history. Yet somehow, Enrique's men seemed more potent with their South American strikeforce.

"If you look at the experiences and the finances, we shouldn't really be on the same pitch as them," said Rodgers before Celtic's Champions League opener at the Camp Nou. "That's the brutal honesty of it. But it shouldn't stop us believing that we can get a result. If you can keep the score at 0-0 for 15 to 20 minutes, you have a big chance, but that's easier said than done."

That was a major understatement. Celtic conceded in the third minute as Messi pounced to kick off a 7-0 defeat for Rodgers' team, the club's heaviest ever European loss. The Argentine genius scored a hat-trick, Suarez got two and Neymar and Andres Iniesta also netted.

From Barca's perspective, the goals were sublime – full of quick passing, skill, movement and deadly finishing. Yet Celtic made it far too easy for them. For Messi's second goal, there were eight defenders surrounding the Barca forward and Neymar on their waltz into the box, but they still managed to manufacture a simple finish from two yards. When Iniesta volleyed in the fourth from 16 yards, seven Celtic players were inside the box and nobody got close to him.

It was a procession from start to finish. Moussa Dembele missed a penalty for Celtic at 1-0 but it's unlikely that would have made a difference. Celtic didn't get near their illustrious opponents in a complete mismatch.

Stung by a rare La Liga defeat to minnows Alaves on the previous weekend, Barca turned on the style to devastating effect against Celtic. Playing the brand of football Rodgers had admired for so long, Enrique's men were irresistible as they scored five goals in the second half.

It was a painful defeat for Celtic but Rodgers defended his players in the face of major criticism for a strangely passive performance in the Camp Nou. "I'm not going to ridicule them and play down what their achievement has been to qualify for the group stages," he said.

Yet, both publicly and privately, he was clear to stress that Celtic could not afford a repeat of the timid display against the world's best players. The difference in quality was apparent but Barcelona had not been made to work for their win. In fact, they had it far too easy.

Rodgers coaches his players to press collectively. It has been a hallmark of all his teams and he spends hours working on this aspect of the game on the training pitch. "If you give a bad player time, he can play, if you give a good player time, he can kill you," is Rodgers' viewpoint.

"You need to be competitive, and in a way that allows you to express yourself. You can sit off and suffer and sit in the box for 85 minutes, but I like to be the aggressor. If you stand off good players they will run rings round you all day. But how good can they be if you go right up against them?

"Every now and then they will earn their £200k per week and play around you a couple of times. That's okay. But next time, let's see if they can do it again and earn their money. If you wait, then you will never become a team."

In the Camp Nou, Celtic barely managed to get up close and personal with the world superstars they faced, committing just three fouls all night. It was a surprising stat and one that irked Rodgers. With such little aggression to their play, the Celtic manager conceded his team never stood a chance against a rampant Barcelona.

Rodgers operated with five defenders and looked to stretch the hosts down the wings by playing Patrick Roberts and Scott Sinclair either side of central striker Dembele. That left Nir Bitton and Scott Brown in central midfield, with full-backs Kieran Tierney and surprise debutant Cristian Gamboa asked to push on if possible.

Yet an inability to keep the ball or win it back killed the plan stone dead. Celtic, fatigued after the win over Rangers three days earlier, were left chasing shadows, especially in the second half.

"If you look at us domestically, in the league and cups, we're a physical team," said Rodgers as he explained where it all went wrong. "We're aggressive in our running and pressing, getting up to people and touching them when we press.

"But the reality is, at Champions League level, in some areas of the field, we don't have the physicality to press the game like we do domestically. Against Barcelona, we weren't aggressive enough."

For the Celtic players, losing 7-0 in the Camp Nou

Brendan Rodgers takes the acclaim from the Celtic supporters as he is unveiled as the club's new manager on May 23, 2016. Around 13,000 fans turned up at Celtic Park to greet him on his first day

Celtic players follow Brendan Rodgers down a path towards their training pitch in Maribor at the start of their pre-season trip, a four-game tour of Slovenia and Austria

Lincoln Red Imps duo Roy Chipolina and Lee Casciaro celebrate their shock 1-0 Champions League qualifier win over Celtic in Gibraltar on July 12

Celtic captain Scott Brown launches himself in celebration after scoring the fifth goal in the 5-2 Champions League first leg play-off win over Hapoel Be'er Sheva

Brendan Rodgers hugs assistant manager Chris Davies at full-time in Celtic's 5-4 aggregate
Champions League play-off win over Hapoel Be'er Sheva, as coach John Kennedy celebrates

Scott Brown takes a selfie with Celtic fans in the background after reaching the Champions League
group stages against Hapoel Be'er Sheva. Celtic lost 2-0 on the night but progressed 5-4 on aggregate

Left: Scott Brown glares at Joey Barton as the Celtic captain goes off injured late in their 5-1 win over Rangers on September 10. The Englishman had claimed Brown wasn't in the same league as him after moving to Ibrox, but was dominated by the Celtic midfielder

Below: Moussa Dembele celebrates the third goal of a perfect hat-trick in Celtic's 5-1 win over Rangers on September 10. The French striker only played because of an injury to Leigh Griffiths but took his chance to make history

Lionel Messi hammers in Barcelona's first goal in a 7-0 win over Celtic in the first Champions League group game on September 13. The Argentine genius scored a hat-trick at the Camp Nou

Brendan Rodgers shares a touchline with Pep Guardiola during Celtic's 3-3 Champions League draw with Man City on September 28. The Celtic manager has been a long-term admirer of the former Barcelona coach and savoured a deserved point for his side

Kieran Tierney celebrates after his cross is diverted in by Raheem Sterling to put Celtic ahead for a second time against Man City. Tierney had been a ballboy at Champions League games in the past

Moussa Dembele hooks in Celtic's third goal in the 3-3 Champions League draw with Man City on September 28. The French striker tormented Pep Guardiola's experienced defence

Left: Stuart Armstrong leads Celtic out as captain for a Premiership fixture against Dundee on December 17. The armband was a symbol of the midfielder's incredible transformation under Brendan Rodgers' guidance

Below: Scott Sinclair celebrates his winning goal against Rangers at Ibrox on New Year's Eve. Celtic had trailed to Kenny Miller's early opener but Moussa Dembele equalised and Sinclair tapped in the winner from Stuart Armstrong's cross

Mikael Lustig performs a rabona pass to help set up Moussa Dembele's hat-trick goal in a 5-2 win over St Johnstone on February 5. Every Celtic player touched the ball in a 25-pass build-up and it was voted PFA Scotland Goal of the Season

Brendan Rodgers pays tribute to captain Scott Brown as he makes his 400th Celtic appearance in a Premiership match against St Johnstone on January 25

was the harshest of lessons but one they ultimately had to learn from quickly. Barcelona had outclassed better teams than Celtic in the past and would go on to score a further 14 home goals against Manchester City, Borussia Monchengladbach and PSG in the competition. Yet captain Brown had no interest in excuses as he reiterated the points made by his manager and told some home truths to his team-mates.

"They're the best team in the world, there's no doubting that," said Brown. "But we need to defend better from the front, midfield and the back. We've got to be a lot more compact and braver on the ball. To lose five goals in the second half was unacceptable."

Brown wasn't as diplomatic in the privacy of an angry dressing room but the Celtic players didn't need to be told that they'd fallen below the standards expected. A few months later, Erik Sviatchenko disclosed just how pivotal that humbling Camp Nou experience was for their development as a team.

"The most important thing is that we don't have the mindset that we are just happy to be in the competition," said the Danish defender. "Some people can be star-struck when you come up against opponents that you play the FIFA computer game with, but you have to forget about that.

"We may be up against bigger teams and better players, but sometimes it's about the preparation and belief. If you believe you can take the ball off Suarez, you will do it. If you are afraid of him, he will probably go past you. That could have been part of the problem in Barcelona – we showed them too much respect."

Celtic took no points from their Camp Nou visit but ultimately, it can be classed as one of the defining games of the season. The importance of that humiliating defeat cannot be underestimated. It was crucial to what followed and the continued development of the team's style.

Rodgers learned a valuable lesson about the capabilities of his squad and just how much improvement was still required. At the same time, his players realised they had to increase their performance levels, to reach the high standards demanded by their manager.

On the ball, Celtic were improving and their extra quality shone in Scotland on a weekly basis. But off the ball, the new manager wanted them to be fitter, faster and stronger, both mentally and physically. On the European scene, against better players, this collective strength was vital. Without it, Celtic were going to be outclassed.

Celtic had come a long way in a short period of time but as the manager could testify from his regular visits to Spain, you can always learn from the elite.

There was little time, though. Manchester City were up next in Group C at Celtic Park, just a fortnight later. Now coached by Guardiola, they had won their first 10 matches under the new manager. It was a daunting prospect for a Celtic side still getting to grips with life at the highest level, but Rodgers' players were determined to show they were quick learners.

CUM ON FEEL THE NOIZE

L IAM GALLAGHER is notoriously selective with his Tweets. The one-time Oasis frontman has over 1.5 million followers on the social media platform but only shares the odd, unique observation with the world.

His amusing, sometimes cryptic, comments are mostly acerbic digs at his estranged brother and former bandmate Noel, or praise for his beloved Manchester City, and 'Sergeant' Pep Guardiola, the club's manager.

At 9.34pm on Wednesday, September 28, 2016, the British music icon abandoned his usual Twitter policy. Moments after the end of an epic 3-3 Champions League draw between Celtic and City, Gallagher felt moved to post the following Tweet.

'What a game of football respect to all those Celtic fans what a sound CUM ON FEEL THE NOIZE LG x'.

Ignoring the lack of punctuation, the Oasis legend perfectly summed up an enthralling, booming evening of European football that will live long in the memory of everyone who witnessed it. Celtic only had a point to show for their efforts against City but this was the night a team came of age under Brendan Rodgers.

Two weeks after their 7-0 humbling from Barcelona, Celtic were a different beast against Guardiola's superstars. The passive nature of their Camp Nou performance was replaced by raw aggression and plenty of skill.

Celtic went toe-to-toe with the English Premier League leaders and although there were some scary moments for Rodgers' defence late on, they came out with their heads held high.

It was a huge effort and Celtic's display didn't go unnoticed across British football and beyond. There was a renewed respect for Scotland's champions after they delivered a level of performance many believed to be beyond them.

Rodgers' Celtic were the first team to halt City and Guardiola seemed both bewildered and inspired by events on the pitch and the noisy soundtrack from the packed Celtic Park stands.

"It was an amazing environment," he said, while wrongly referring to his opponents as 'Glasgow the Celtic' and 'Celtic of Glasgow' in a confusing, amusing post-match interview.

Rodgers was more controlled and composed. He was naturally disappointed not to win the game after Celtic had led three times but admitted that, like Guardiola, he was left in awe at the spectacle and atmosphere.

"It was a noise I've never heard before," he said. "It was a special night. When you come to Celtic Park for these games, you realise why many players around the world talk about the atmosphere here. The fans really helped us to produce the performance we did." In the Celtic Park boardroom, supporters and celebrities queued up to congratulate Rodgers on the impressive progress made by a Celtic team that had lost twice to Norwegian minnows Molde just 12 months previously in the Europa League. Among them was the other Gallagher brother, Noel.

The singer-songwriter had never hidden his affection for Celtic or Rodgers, memorably christening him 'The Brodge' during a Match of the Day 2 appearance in early 2015. Months later, he also labelled the-then Liverpool manager a "superhero" during a Sky Sports interview.

"The people I spoke to after the game, celebrities, said they had never heard anything like it," said Rodgers. "I spoke to Noel, who I've bumped into a few times at City. The last game he was at here was the 6-2 game against Rangers under Martin O'Neill and he said the City game was at another level in terms of noise."

For days following the City fixture, the Celtic Park atmosphere continued to receive praise in the football world but Rodgers was committed to looking at the 3-3 draw in silence, in order to delve deeper into the positives and negatives of his team's performance and progress.

Defensively, it was clear Celtic remained suspect at Champions League level. They had now shipped 10 goals in two games, albeit against arguably the two leading teams in Europe at that point of the season. Had Craig Gordon not produced a heroic save in the final seconds, City would have won.

Along with two-goal Moussa Dembele, it was an inspired individual performance from the Scotland goalkeeper. Yet it was the collective effort from Celtic that pleased Rodgers the most and demonstrated to the manager that the lessons of the Barcelona defeat had been taken on board. There was work to be done but the signs were positive.

From start to finish, Celtic played like a Rodgers team in every sense, pressing their opponents relentlessly and displaying quality and invention on the ball. That it came against a Guardiola team, a man Rodgers had admired for years, only heightened his pride at the performance.

"We started the City game with great intensity," said Rodgers. "For us it was about tactically setting up and pressing. It has to be an educated pressure because if not they will run through you. There were many examples of counter pressing. That's an example of working collectively very hard.

"If you are not organised against this City team, like we've seen in the Premier League they can really hurt you. It was a big step forward for us. We put down a marker.

"Celtic is one of the biggest clubs in the world. It just doesn't have the platform of the Premier League. To come and virtually out-press Manchester City? The players deserve the respect for that."

Celtic would end their Champions League campaign with another impressive performance and 1-1 draw against City at the Etihad as they exited the competition. In between those two games against the English side, it was a period of learning, progress, but ultimately frustration for Rodgers and his players.

Barcelona won 2-0 at Celtic Park in November courtesy of a Lionel Messi double but it was the outcome of the double-header with Borussia Monchengladbach that proved pivotal as Celtic finished bottom of

Group C and failed to land the consolation of a Europa League knockout place.

Strangely, Rodgers' team performed better in Germany than Glasgow. In the Celtic Park meeting, Monchengladbach were superior all over the pitch. They successfully stifled Celtic's traditional early onslaught, and instead put Rodgers' team on the back foot. This had been coach Andre Schubert's plan and it worked perfectly.

In his pre-match press conference, the German spoke about the "power and passion" of the Celtic fans. He had analysed City's visit to Celtic Park and realised his team could not allow themselves to be caught up in the same whirlwind opening. Instead, Monchengladbach killed the frenzied atmosphere by playing simple passes and retaining the ball. Celtic could not find any rhythm.

Germany midfielder Christoph Kramer was the catalyst for everything. He sat deep and dictated the play. Monchengladbach continually attacked down the right wing, intentionally pinning Kieran Tierney back in his own half, and Celtic never recovered from a poor start. Defensive frailties haunted them as Lars Stindl and Andre Hahn scored second-half goals. Rodgers had no complaints at the outcome. "They were a level above us," he said.

Given the paucity of their home performance, Celtic arrived in Germany two weeks later with a point to prove. They did that and were unfortunate to leave with only a 1-1 draw after an accomplished display full of confidence and poise in Monchengladbach. Celtic's passing was noticeably crisper and they grew in confidence as the game progressed. After Dembele's second-half penalty equaliser, Callum McGregor passed up a gilt-edged late chance to seal the win that Celtic deserved.

The midfielder is normally composed in front of goal but his touch deserted him and he dragged his shot wide after Patrick Roberts had cut open the Monchengladbach defence with a slide-rule pass. Had McGregor scored, Celtic would have finished third in the group and secured a place in the Europa League knockout rounds. It was a defining moment.

Yet Rodgers still spoke of his pride after a mature away display against the Bundesliga team. "It's another step forward in a very short period of time," he said. "We're trying to create a team that can come to Europe, be a real threat and play with composure and bravery. We should've won the game. I thought we were the best team."

For Celtic, the point in Germany at least made up for that performance against Monchengladbach on home soil. The Germans' two second-half goals were gifted to them by glaring Kolo Toure errors. It was the beginning of the end for the Ivorian as a first-team regular, who owned up to making "16-year-old's mistakes". Toure had been nursing an injury during that period and Rodgers removed him from the firing line, allowing Jozo Simunovic to take on a more prominent role in central defence.

Toure had done his job in helping Celtic reach the group stages and Rodgers continued to value his influential presence around the squad. Yet there was no room for sentiment when it came to picking his team. With Simunovic progressing and Dedryck Boyata blossoming, Rodgers had more defensive options as the season progressed. Toure started just one more game.

Invincible

Rodgers knew his players hadn't done themselves justice against the Germans in Glasgow, but the final three fixtures of the campaign reinforced his belief that they were on the right track. By the time the final whistle blew at the Etihad, Rodgers spoke with positivity about the entire Champions League experience.

"Take away the monetary side, it's about learning in this environment, and you can't put a price on that," he said. "They became better players in every aspect of the game. We could have beaten City in both games and that sets the standard for us.

"We have grown and developed, and this is what this year was probably going to be about. We were competing against superpowers in European football. In the main, our performance levels were very good."

Reminded of his first European game in charge of Celtic, against Lincoln Red Imps, Rodgers also conceded that the infamous Gibraltar defeat in July arguably proved to be a blessing in disguise for his players.

"I think that game was a nice little wake-up call for them," he said. "There had been a lot of the good work done over the pre-season, but that showed me there was still a way to go with these players in terms of belief, that they could actually go out there and lose a game like that.

"It can happen with the astro pitch and everything else. But it sharpened the teeth in many aspects of what we wanted to do. It also told me a couple of wee things early on about the fragility of the team and what we had to improve."

These views were echoed by the Celtic players. Captain Scott Brown is the club's most experienced Champions League player and was well placed to comment on their progress. "We've followed the gaffer's philosophy," he said. "We were a bit slow in starting it against Barcelona, we couldn't have got off to a worse start, but as soon as we did get going, everything has gradually come together." Leigh Griffiths followed on a similar theme: "From the start of the campaign to the end, it's been like two different teams."

Rodgers agreed but immediately set ambitious targets as he began plotting a Champions League return for his team in 2017/18 and beyond. "I would hope Celtic are a last-16 team in two or three years' time," he said. "It is step by step. We were in the toughest group in the competition and it was difficult for us. But we don't see it as a threat. We see it as a challenge.

"That was the aim for me coming here, to really build the club and for us to qualify for the Champions League and to get out of the group stages and see how far we can go there."

Gibraltar, Kazakhstan, the Israeli desert, Lionel Messi, Liam, Noel and Pep. It had been a hell of a ride. As Celtic headed north home from the Etihad the message on board the team coach was simple: Let's make sure we do it all over again next season.

MOUSSA DEMBELE
THE WOLF OF KERRYDALE STREET

ROYAL GARDEN hotel, Kensington. Late May 2016. Brendan Rodgers is in full flow. "We can call Luis Suarez. He'll tell you what I am like as a manager, what I can do for you." Moussa Dembele glances at his agent, Mamadi Fofana. "I want to make a statement. I want you to be my first signing for Celtic."

Dembele is in demand across Europe at this point. Only 19, the Fulham striker is out of contract after scoring 17 goals in season 2015/16. PSG and Juventus are tracking him. The French teenager had almost signed for Tottenham Hotspur four months earlier and Mauricio Pochettino retains an interest. Astronomical wages are on the table from a variety of suitors.

Many players of Dembele's age and potential wouldn't

even consider Celtic and Scottish football. He could go to a better league, for better money. He could secure a life-changing contract in England, Italy or France and safeguard his financial future with one stroke of a pen. Yet Dembele has a different outlook. Short-term financial gain is tempting, but he is intent on playing the long game with his career. However, will the long game take him to Celtic?

The input of Dembele's agent is crucial. Together they had drawn up a checklist for his next club. There are three main points. Dembele needs regular first-team football, he needs to play under pressure and expectation, and he needs exposure to European football. If it's the Champions League? Perfect. But even the Europa League will aid his development.

But most importantly, Dembele must work with a manager who believes in him. Someone who can nurture his talent and take his game to the next level. The teenager will only sign for a club after looking into the whites of his new manager's eyes. He doesn't want to be signed by a sporting director and presented to a head coach. This is a deal-breaker. Dembele is clear on that.

Celtic hold a long-standing interest and tick every box. David Moss, a first-team scout in John Park's successful recruitment operation, has tracked the French striker for the bulk of the previous season. He delivered glowing reports and Ronny Deila spoke to Fofana after Dembele entered the final six months of his Fulham contract.

In the free market, he is rated at around £8million by the Championship club. If Dembele goes to another English club, they will urge the Professional Football Compensation Committee to determine a fee of millions. But under FIFA rules, Celtic only need to pay minimal training compensation to sign him on a cross-border transfer.

Enter Rodgers. The new Celtic manager is fully aware of Dembele's quality and believes he can become a powerful focal point for his new-look team. Rodgers is keen to meet the teenager and offer an insight into his plans. Celtic book a private conference room in the Royal Garden and the manager hosts a meal for Dembele, Fofana and his cousin and business partner, Makan Fofana.

They eat and chat about Dembele's background and his ambitions. Rodgers is keen to learn the player's career goals before he outlines his long-term vision for Celtic. He writes on a flipchart, illustrating where he wants Dembele to play. Rodgers already knows his game inside out and promises to develop his strengths and work on his weaknesses. He looks at Dembele and tells him he can help him become one of the best strikers in the world.

The Celtic manager discusses his own career. He talks at length about Suarez at Liverpool and offers Dembele the chance to make a call to the Barcelona striker. Rodgers makes reference to Raheem Sterling, Daniel Sturridge and all the other young players he has helped develop in his long coaching career.

Rodgers leaves after a two-hour meeting. Dembele is quiet, reflective. He is facing the biggest decision of his career. After a few moments, his agent speaks: "What do you think?"

"I have a good feeling about Celtic," says Dembele.
"So do I."
Dembele looks at Fofana and nods. "Let's make it

happen." By June 11, Dembele's representatives were at Lennoxtown for further talks as a deal neared completion. Fulham were due a fee of around £500,000 in training compensation. His wages put him among the club's highest earners, but Rodgers and the Celtic board sensed they were getting a bargain. On June 28, his signing was confirmed. Dembele would become one of the biggest coups in the club's history. The London summit with Rodgers had been pivotal.

"Meeting Brendan made the difference," said Fofana. "I'm not being disrespectful to other managers but when Brendan Rodgers tells a player how much he wants him, it is a major compliment. Financially, Moussa could have earned more elsewhere but Celtic was the right club for him. It was the time to be wise and learn."

Dembele is not short of confidence. On his first day as a Celtic player, he laid out his lofty personal ambitions and promised the fans that he would help the team qualify for the Champions League group stages. "I want to become one of the best strikers or the best striker in the world," said Dembele. "Hopefully I can score as many goals as I can for Celtic and become like Henrik Larsson. To be Brendan Rodgers' first signing is unreal."

Patience was initially required from Dembele, who operated in the shadow of Leigh Griffiths in the early part of the season. The Celtic striker had scored 40 goals in 2015/16 and was the first choice if Rodgers operated with one central forward. Griffiths started with seven goals in nine games and was determined to protect his status. Dembele had missed a chunk of pre-season and Rodgers allowed him to find his fitness and ease his way in.

Yet there were early signs of Dembele's precocious

talent. He came off the bench to win and score the penalty against Astana at Celtic Park, and earn a play-off against Hapoel Be'er Sheva. The teenager then scored his side's vital fourth goal against the Israelis in the 5-2 first-leg home win, powering in a header from Griffiths' corner. He was already proving to be a big-game player by the time September 10 arrived.

Celtic 5 Rangers 1. A game that changed Dembele's life forever. It wasn't just his perfect hat-trick that caught the eye, it was the way he tormented the Rangers backline with a mixture of pace and power. He had turned 20 by then and produced a complete performance that belied his age. Dembele only started due to an injury to Griffiths but within 90 minutes he had become a Celtic hero.

It was only the start. Dembele missed a penalty in Celtic's following game, a 7-0 defeat to Barcelona, but in their next Champions League outing, a 3-3 draw with Manchester City at Celtic Park, he produced arguably his best display of the season, on the biggest stage. It was the night Dembele truly announced himself to the football world.

Dembele diverted Erik Sviatchenko's header over the line to give Celtic an early lead and then scored an acrobatic volley in the second half. City's central defenders Nicolas Otamendi and Aleksandar Kolarov appeared terrified of him. "Moussa bullied the City back four," said Rodgers. "He showed pace, power and agility. He was outstanding." Pep Guardiola agreed. "Dembele is exceptional," was his succinct assessment.

Dembele continued to progress at a rapid rate. He scored 20 goals before the winter break, including a Betfred Cup semi-final winner over Rangers and the thumping volley for Celtic's equaliser in the 2-1 New Year's Eve victory at Ibrox. Towards the end of that Premiership fixture, Rangers players bounced off him as he protected the ball and wasted time at the corner flag.

The Celtic striker also scored penalties against Aberdeen in the Betfred Cup final and against Borussia Monchengladbach in the 1-1 away Champions League draw. He continued to thrive on the big stage and his progress was noted across Europe. Two eye-catching goals for France under-21s against England in November only heightened the hype surrounding him.

"Moussa is a big-game player and that's why he'll have a really good career," said Rodgers. "He always turns up in the big games because he has that motivation. That's what top players do, they live for the big games. You can see it in him. Having worked with senior players at that level before, you need that personality and belief in abundance. He can go into cauldrons and big games with big pressure and take it on, embrace it and love it. It's a personality trait and Moussa has it."

Scouts followed Dembele closely as the January transfer window approached. Guardiola refused to rule out a move, while Chelsea were the most heavily linked. Rodgers remained adamant his prized asset was not for sale and shot down any suggestions that Celtic could cash in for £15million, which was just higher than the record transfer fee Southampton paid to the club for Virgil van Dijk in 2015. "£15million? That's for Moussa's left toe," said the Celtic manager, only half joking.

Rodgers compared Dembele's style of play to former Chelsea striker Didier Drogba and for 24 hours towards the end of January it looked like the Celtic player could be heading to Stamford Bridge, with talk of a £40million transfer. It said everything about Dembele's growing reputation that this size of fee wasn't automatically dismissed.

Celtic's £500,000 investment in Dembele looked certain to bring a major return one day, but the club continued to deny receiving any bids. Yet the speculation became frenzied on the afternoon of January 31. Dembele boarding a flight to London to visit a knee specialist in the Chelsea area only increased the transfer talk, but the player himself then killed it all off with one simple Tweet at 5.57pm that day.

Dembele posted an image that showed him in the same arms-outstretched pose as Leonardo DiCaprio in The Wolf of Wall Street, during the scene where he announces to his staff, "I'm not fucking leaving". He opted against posting the expletive-laden film clip due to the many youngsters who follow him on Twitter but still managed to get his message across. Dembele was going nowhere.

The Celtic striker was aware that bids of £40million would be almost impossible for his club to turn down but in Dembele's mind, nothing had changed from the day he met Rodgers in London. He was still convinced Celtic was the best place for his long-term development, playing at a big club and working under a manager who could guarantee him games and had already helped improve him.

"It's easy not to get distracted," said Dembele. "I'm a very calm kind of guy and I don't really let this type of thing get in my head. I focus only on enjoying my football at Celtic and I'm very happy to be here. The talk is flattering and it motivates me to keep doing well."

On February 1, Dembele was back at Lennoxtown,

working under Rodgers' supervision. The Celtic manager continued to develop all aspects of the striker's game. He saw room for improvement in his movement, pressing, finishing and game intelligence. Could Dembele's link-up play get better? Could he be even more clinical in the box? Those were the challenges Rodgers gave him.

The Celtic striker accepted them. Returning from injury, he wasn't deemed fit enough to start against St Johnstone on February 5 but came off the bench to score a 24-minute hat-trick in a 5-2 win. That kicked off a run of 12 goals in six games for Dembele, including another treble against Inverness Caledonian Thistle. His improved awareness was evident during this period. Dembele's hold-up play had become more accomplished as the extra work on the training ground continued to pay off.

By March 5, after scoring against St Mirren in the Scottish Cup, Dembele was on 32 goals for the season with almost three months remaining. France coach Didier Deschamps talked him up as an international player of the future. At that stage, he was widely expected to break Griffiths' 40-goal return for the previous season.

It never happened, with injury ending the striker's season prematurely. He had only just returned from a minor hamstring strain when he pulled up again during Celtic's 2-0 Scottish Cup semi-final win over Rangers. He suffered a Grade 2 tear and was ruled out for five weeks, effectively ending his campaign. Fittingly, Dembele's last act was to pluck Mikael Lustig's long pass out of the sky and expertly set up Callum McGregor for Celtic's first goal at Hampden.

Dembele finished his debut season at Celtic with 32 goals and nine assists in 49 appearances. He was nominated for the Scottish PFA's Player of the Year and Young Player of the Year awards and established a reputation as one of the best young strikers in European football. The £500,000 paid to Fulham was Celtic's best piece of business since signing Larsson from Feyenoord for £650,000 in 1997.

A SUITCASE FULL
OF DREAMS

SCOTT BROWN scanned Celtic's fixture list for
November and December, and realised he had a
minor problem. As club captain, the midfielder has
many responsibilities, one of which is to organise the
team Christmas night out. Yet finding a date for the 2016
festivities was proving problematic.

In the modern world of smartphones and social
media, very few football teams stay in their home city
for the annual Christmas outing. Legendary tales of
Celtic's centenary season squad doing shuttle runs in
fancy dress along Glasgow's Sauchiehall Street around
Christmas 1987 spoke of a more innocent era. In those
days, players could gather in a local pub, knock back a
few drinks and nobody would bother them.

Times have changed. Most football teams across
Britain now hold their festive gatherings outside city
boundaries. For years, Celtic had opted to travel to
England for a night out followed by the traditional fancy

dress day. In 2016, London was the players' choice, but a congested fixture list provided just one window of opportunity.

Football always comes first. Brown knew Celtic could only pencil in their Christmas bonding trip if they had no midweek match in the days following. But with 12 games in a six-week period in the lead up to Christmas, the only possible date of departure was Sunday, November 27: the day of Celtic's Betfred Cup final meeting with Aberdeen at Hampden.

Brown speaks daily to manager Brendan Rodgers and raised the topic of the squad's London outing and the possibility of getting two days off after the final. The Celtic manager had no issue with his players going away to hopefully celebrate their first trophy of the season, but naturally wanted to ensure full focus ahead of such an important fixture.

Rodgers gave Brown the go-ahead to arrange the Christmas party, with certain conditions. The Celtic captain agreed to them and on Thursday, November 24, the morning after playing Barcelona in the Champions League, the players who had signed up for London arrived at Lennoxtown one by one, armed with suitcases containing their clothes for the trip.

The luggage was collected by Celtic's kitmen and placed in storage for 72 hours. Rodgers didn't want to even glimpse the London cases, filled with designer clothes, in the team hotel ahead of the cup final. The Celtic players wouldn't see their belongings again until they had beaten Aberdeen. If they lost at Hampden, the suitcases would stay in the kit van, the plane tickets would remain unused.

Rodgers' players parked all thoughts of the Christmas

party. Their sole focus was on winning the first trophy of the season and the 100th major honour in Celtic's history.

As the Celtic squad strolled out onto the Hampden pitch in green New Balance tracksuits they looked like a team ready to go to work. In contrast, the Aberdeen party looked far more dapper in their grey suit trousers and navy blazers, with flowers on the lapel. But Rodgers and his players knew the final was about substance, not style.

The Celtic manager intentionally kept the pre-match routine exactly the same as normal. While the Aberdeen squad spent two days in St Andrews before moving to a Glasgow base on the eve of the game, Celtic prepared as they would for any other game. This helped alleviate any added pressure ahead of the biggest domestic fixture of the season up to that point.

Gathering his players and staff together in the Hampden dressing room before kick-off, Rodgers spoke about Celtic's past, present and future. He told them they could follow in the footsteps of legends and win the club's 100th major trophy; he spoke about the progress they had made in the first half of the season and how this was the chance to mark the start of a new era with a trophy. In closing, he urged the Celtic players to be on that Hampden podium celebrating at the end.

Celtic reached the Betfred Cup final without conceding a goal, beating Motherwell, Alloa and Rangers to get there. Moussa Dembele's clever flick secured a 1-0 win over Mark Warburton's team in the semi-final but the scoreline didn't reflect Celtic's dominance. "The performance was the same as the 5-1 win in September," said Rodgers. "We just didn't finish our opportunities." By the time of the final, Celtic were playing some of their best football of the season. Players like Stuart Armstrong were emerging, yet the volume of domestic and European games had started to take its toll. Rodgers was without the injured Kieran Tierney and Scott Sinclair for the Aberdeen match. In their absence, the Celtic manager needed others to accept extra responsibility.

Nobody did this more than Tom Rogic. The elegant Australian attacking midfielder was plagued by injury after being signed by Neil Lennon in January 2013 and suffered a false start to his Celtic career. Yet Rogic fought back to full fitness during Ronny Deila's reign and, like so many of his team-mates, took his game to another level under Rodgers' guidance.

The Australian was a late developer, earning his first professional contract with A-League club Central Coast Mariners aged 19 after winning 'The Chance' – a talent competition run by Nike. Rogic had been a leading futsal player for his country and his nimble footwork and graceful style transferred successfully to 11-a-side football.

Rodgers nicknamed him Celtic's 'Magic Man'. He was mesmerised by Rogic's natural ability and convinced him to sign a new contract within two months of taking over. "Tom's an amazing player and can grow into one of the top midfield players in Europe," said Rodgers. "There's no doubt he's top class. Top players know where the space is and Tom's as good as any I've seen at finding it."

Aberdeen midfielder Graeme Shinnie can testify to that. He tracked Rogic's run to the right angle of the box at Hampden but it took just one swivel of the Australian's hips to find a yard and bend a left-foot shot beyond goalkeeper Joe Lewis to put Celtic ahead. For the second goal, Rogic proved similarly elusive as he again worked his way past Shinnie in a tight space to set James Forrest free for a devastatingly direct run and finish.

Celtic didn't have a single failure as they outclassed Aberdeen in a comfortable 3-0 win but Rogic stood out. His finesse and weight of pass allowed Forrest to glide into the box and win a penalty in the second half. Dembele converted and Rodgers secured his first trophy as Celtic manager as the club reached a significant landmark.

"Celtic is a winning club," said Rodgers. "That is what the history of this great club has been based upon. This cup marks a milestone, that century of trophies over the course of history. Now we have got to look to the next one and start off the next century of trophies."

Rodgers walked up the Hampden steps after his players and was the last man to hold the trophy aloft. The cheers got even louder when Brown raised the cup on the pitch just in time for a spectacular fireworks display. The captain had produced a commanding performance in midfield and also played a pivotal role as he led the traditional pre-match Celtic huddle with some final words of encouragement.

"The importance of the occasion was reiterated to us before the game," said Celtic winger Patrick Roberts. "When we went into the huddle on the pitch, Broony spoke to us about that. For a guy like him to talk with such raw passion in the huddle was lovely.

"He told us we had a chance to make history by winning the 100th trophy and how much that would mean. Scott's been through everything at Celtic and he knows exactly what it means. He's been in that position so many times and made sure we were all aware of what was at stake.

"It was great to hear his words before the game and it really motivated us to go out and win. As soon as that whistle went, we were all determined to show what we are capable of. We did that, we got that 100th trophy and it was a special day for everyone involved."

After a lingering lap of honour, Rodgers and his Celtic players were joined in the dressing room by Dermot Desmond, Peter Lawwell and several board members, who posed for photographs and took part in more celebrations. Bottles of champagne were popped as Kolo Toure led the Kolo/Yaya chant and dance made famous by Man City supporters.

After the suitcases were delivered, the players heading off for the Christmas outing in London showered and changed into their own clothes. Once all media duties had been completed, a bus arrived to take them to Glasgow Airport. The rest joined Rodgers and the backroom staff on the journey back to Celtic Park, where hundreds of fans were waiting to greet them.

Celtic had prepared for winning a historic century of trophies, with huge neon letters bearing 'CFC 100' set up at the stadium entrance. Rodgers got another massive ovation as he emerged out the front door with Tierney to show off the trophy to the fans gathered behind the steel barriers outside Celtic Park on a cold November night.

It was after 7pm when Rodgers stepped up to a microphone to address those supporters. Standing in the shadow of Jock Stein's imposing statue, between 'CFC' and '100', he sat the Betfred Cup down beside him and made a short speech after the cheers finally died down.

"On behalf of the staff and myself, we just want to

give a huge thank you, because we do it for you – the supporters," said Rodgers. "The plan coming into the club was to roll out a vision that would keep us all together, players, supporters, so that we could connect.

"Today is six months and just over a week since I arrived in here. The plan was to grow together and improve our football on the pitch. But also the mark of that was going to be, could we then win and get onto the podium? Today we did that.

"We played very well in the game but I also must give the supporters a big thank you. As manager of a club I've supported all my life, to win that first trophy means a lot to us. But it obviously means everything to you too. So thank you very much and enjoy your night."

Rodgers was almost overcome with emotion towards the end of his speech, with his late parents Malachy and Christina never far from his thoughts. "I had a flashback of something that was important to me," he later explained. "I just wished some people who aren't here anymore were there."

The Betfred Cup was a major step forward for Rodgers. The Hampden success gave the manager and his entire Celtic staff something tangible to show for their work in the first six months of his reign. There was a sense of achievement as the party inside Celtic Park began to hit full swing but Rodgers was content to slip away quietly with his family.

"I was home at 8.30pm," he said. "I had a drink with the directors and spoke to the staff at Celtic. I then went home for a cup of tea and a bit of toast, and watched the game again.

"I'm not a big drinker. I was teetotal until my early 20s, and my parents never drank. That's not to say there's

Invincible

anything wrong in celebrating with a drink. We do it in different ways. Some players decided to go for a meal, some decided to go and have a real good time. I said to them to make sure they went away and had a couple of days to really enjoy it."

That's what Brown and his team-mates did. As Rodgers was settling down to his tea and toast to watch a replay of the game, they were touching down in London, with suitcases in hand.

ADAPT AND FLY

"I always say to the players: 'It's your responsibility. The crown is on your head. You are the king of your own destiny. Wherever you go is down to you'."
Brendan Rodgers, October 13, 2016

Commitment
Organisation
Responsibility
Excellence

STUART ARMSTRONG stared at the four words as Brendan Rodgers began to talk. What followed was the most important conversation of the midfielder's career.

It was early in the 2016/17 season and Armstrong was at a crossroads. He was in and out of the Celtic team, unable to nail down a regular place. He was a central midfielder constantly being pushed to the fringes of the action on the left wing, hindered by his own versatility.

Inconsistency and a series of niggling injuries had largely written off the previous season for the player. Armstrong had made a dynamic start at Celtic following his £1.8million move from Dundee United in February 2015 but his career had stalled unexpectedly.

Yet Rodgers saw glimpses of quality in the former Scotland under-21 captain. He was watching Celtic's 7-0 win over Motherwell on television on May 15 when Armstrong produced a moment of mesmerising elegance to volley in the fourth goal.

After being appointed the following week, the new manager analysed every goal Celtic scored and conceded in the 2015/16 season. Armstrong's flashes stood out as Rodgers worked through the footage. The understated brilliance of his delicate cross for Kris Commons' acrobatic finish against Dundee United on January 15 was another telling cameo.

Rodgers could see there was something special about Armstrong. His task was to unlock this potential. He had to settle on the versatile midfielder's best position and allow him to flourish. Aged 24, this was going to be the defining season in his career.

Shortly after pre-season training began, Rodgers arranged the one-to-one meeting with Armstrong. He asked his player to be honest about his frustrations from the past, and also the ambitions he held for his career, with Celtic and beyond.

The Celtic manager listened to Armstrong make his case for a central position. He was convinced he could help him blossom but he needed the midfielder to put his heart and soul into what he had planned for him and the club. This led Rodgers to his four CORE principles of player development – Commitment, Organisation, Responsibility and Excellence.

Rodgers has spoken about going through this process with first-team players during his managerial career. Age doesn't matter. For the Celtic manager, CORE is about a desire to improve as an individual and become an integral part of the collective. From there, Rodgers will give players the best of everything, from coaching to sports science work and nutrition. But there has to be full buy-in from players, otherwise it doesn't work.

"As long as players are committed, I have a plan for them to be the best they can be," said Rodgers. "But they have to be committed and I don't mean motivation. Motivation is attached to emotion and you are going to be up and down all the time.

"If you're committed, we will organise a plan for you – whatever team sport it is, it's about the individual too. From that, I always say to the players, 'It's your responsibility. The crown is on your head. You are the king of your own destiny. Wherever you go, is down to you'.

"We have the tools that can make them the best they can be and hopefully they then deliver excellence on the field. Hopefully they then represent the club and the team in the best way they can."

Walking out of that meeting with Rodgers, Armstrong felt positive about his Celtic future. His fortunes wouldn't change overnight. There was a lot of work to be done before he would become an automatic choice in central midfield but the Celtic manager promised him a chance.

Rodgers' message to Armstrong was clear: Push

yourself every day. Armstrong had all the attributes
to be a success under Rodgers but it was down to him
to marry talent with application and show his value at
Lennoxtown on a daily basis. Like every member of the
Celtic squad, the crown was on his head.

"Every training session is important," said Rodgers.
"That was something we nailed with the players from the
very first day. Sometimes at big clubs, like Celtic, your
talent can hide you in among other good players.

"You can be hidden and you can be protected a little
bit which means you don't have to work quite so hard
because your ability takes you there. No chance. If
you're not working here you will be out, regardless of
your talent.

"I said it early in my time here that some players
will struggle to keep up. Their talent is there but they
can't keep up with the demand. So your talent won't be
protected. You can be a good player but it's not enough.

"If you want to be elite and you want to be the best,
then you have to align the working mentality with the
talent. That means you push in every single training
session and game."

Rodgers sensed Armstrong could be a No.8 in
his team, a central midfielder who could do a bit of
everything. He outlined the basic tactical requirements
and expectations of that role. Armstrong realised he
needed to be an all-rounder, combining defensive
discipline with attacking creativity as he worked
Rodgers' infield 'corridors' up and down the pitch.

He already had the pace, power and poise for the
position. Rodgers demands that his midfielders are
constantly on the move and are willing to get physical
with their opponents. Armstrong knew improved

strength and fitness were a necessity to help him earn a regular place. The player met the challenge head on.

"The initial conversation about how the manager wanted me to go about my business at Celtic really spurred me on," said Armstrong. "Following that there was a clear picture about what I needed to do to be part of his side. He gave me a great platform and opportunity to work my way into the side and play in my favoured position."

Armstrong grafted in the background but initially continued to drift in and out of the squad as Rodgers evaluated his options, added new signings and tried to maintain a level of consistency in selection and results. But by early September, Armstrong was making inroads.

The midfielder scored Celtic's fifth goal in the 5-1 win over Rangers on September 10. It came at the end of an impressive cameo when he was operating in a central midfield position. It was a big moment for Armstrong and a reward for his hard work and willingness to learn.

By October 23, when Celtic played Rangers in the Betfred Cup semi-final, Armstrong was pushing hard for a regular start. Nir Bitton was chosen ahead him at Hampden but Rodgers sent Armstrong on after 63 minutes. His introduction added zest and aggression to the Celtic midfield. Armstrong pressed Rangers, showed quality on the ball and drove the team on. Another substitute, Leigh Griffiths, set up Moussa Dembele's winner but Armstrong made a massive contribution to the victory.

Everything changed from that point onwards. Armstrong started and scored against Ross County three days later and then became a fixture in the

Celtic midfield. He scored another six goals before the turn of the year and excelled in Champions League games away against Borussia Monchengladbach and Manchester City.

Before Celtic's 2-1 home win over Dundee on December 17, Armstrong's transformation from bit-part squad player to first-team mainstay was complete. With Scott Brown serving a one-match suspension, the midfielder was given the honour of captaining Celtic.

"Making Stu captain was a symbol for him and the other players," said Rodgers. "This was a guy who was a stand-out when I was assessing the squad. Then it was in doubt whether he would play for me. Early in the season he wasn't even in a couple of the squads.

"But guys like Stu epitomise how I work. If they can adapt, they can fly. They get their reward and he has been a great symbol of that. He is outstanding in everything he does."

Armstrong continued to thrive. He won two Player of the Month awards and his exceptional club form was rewarded with a first Scotland cap, against Slovenia in March. He was outstanding as he set up Chris Martin's goal in a 1-0 win, with Gordon Strachan branding his performance "the best Scotland debut ever".

By the end of the season, Armstrong's Player of the Year nomination was a foregone conclusion. The midfielder was the most improved performer in Scottish football by some distance. He scored 17 goals, a variety of shots, headers and free-kicks, and became one of the important players in the Celtic team. His emphatic equaliser in the Scottish Cup final illustrated his influence.

Armstrong was his manager's ideal No.8. His

defensive positioning and awareness had improved and his increased fitness levels allowed him to press harder, for longer. In the bigger games, Armstrong relished the responsibility of partnering Brown in midfield. Against Rangers at Ibrox on New Year's Eve, his driving run and cross to set up Scott Sinclair's winner typified an all-action performance.

Armstrong took huge credit for his own transformation but it was also a victory for Rodgers' coaching nous and ability to get inside his players' heads. The Celtic manager is a huge believer in the importance of sports psychology. At Liverpool, renowned psychiatrist Dr Steve Peters worked closely with his players. Rodgers also studied neuro-linguistic programming (NLP) for five years and knows which buttons to push to get the reaction he wants.

Armstrong's progress was the most dramatic, but others like James Forrest, Tom Rogic, Mikael Lustig and Craig Gordon earned new contracts off the back of improved performances. Jozo Simunovic came back stronger from his injury problems, while fellow defender Dedryck Boyata emerged as a player reborn after the winter break.

Moussa Dembele and Scott Sinclair thrived after joining in the summer of 2016, while teenagers Patrick Roberts and Kieran Tierney continued to develop. Callum McGregor also rose to prominence and became a key player in the final months of the season. Brown's resurrection as captain knitted everything together for Rodgers.

"The psychology part is massive," said the Celtic manager. "I find that part of the game fascinating, in terms of getting the best out of people. A lot of work goes into the technical, the tactical, and obviously the physical side. But the mental aspect is about managing the pressure and the stress, and being consistent. That is obviously the key and I tend to focus on that quite a lot.

"Sometimes pressure is about perception. You get given pressure but it's about how you take it. If you want to be successful, the reality is, it's always there. It never goes away.

"It's my job to help the players come a little bit away from that, and let them focus on the football. I'll take whatever comes with the pressure, so long as they can go out and give their very best.

"I want the players just to enjoy their life at this great football club. I want them to turn up every day and have confidence and optimism. I want them to keep trying to improve, be tenacious, be aggressive, and have enthusiasm.

"If you have that, then it can help you every day in how you approach your work and your life. When the pressure comes, those are good measures for you in how to deal with them.

"NLP is about the neurology of the brain and it's based around that side of football. People talk about sports psychology but there are different types and different emotions to motivate players.

"I enjoy being around people and I enjoy making people feel good. It's how you frame situations and frame negatives. I say to the players, 'If you want a problem, there is one just round the corner'. The world is full of them. Try to find a solution and be the best you can be."

That so many players earned improved contracts in

his first season pleased Rodgers, who acknowledged that, in the modern game especially, money is always a huge motivation. The Celtic manager was happy to talk wage packets with members of his squad. In fact, he encouraged it.

Rodgers reminded his players they had a short career. He spoke about the limited timeframe in which to rake in money before it all comes to an end, and used the prospect of greater financial rewards as motivation for his Celtic squad. The way he saw it, if they were playing at a level that deserved enhanced terms, it could only benefit the player and club.

Disclosing a conversation he had with an unnamed 25-year-old Celtic player, he said: "I was talking to him and I said, 'Between now and 35 you only really have 120 pay packets left. So can we now apply ourselves better, that'll improve performance and then you might just get a little hike in those pay packets that allows you to be the best you can be for you and your family."

It's probably no coincidence that the anecdote was relayed around the time of Boyata's return to the Celtic team in January. The 25-year-old Belgian defender had endured a disappointing first season at the club in 2015/16 and injury limited his chances in the early months of Rodgers' reign. However, he made a strong recovery in the second half of the campaign and eventually established himself as a first choice. It had been a long road for the Celtic defender, but Rodgers held Boyata up as an example of what dedication could achieve.

"When Dedryck wasn't in the squad for games he'd come back to Lennoxtown and he'd be working in the gym to midnight and beyond," said Rodgers. "He worked hard and was patient, and I always say to the players, 'The door will open for you, just be ready to come through it.'"

FOLLOW THE STAR

THE giant gold star was placed above Celtic Park's main entrance just before Christmas. It was never taken down. Fittingly, it became a permanent symbol for the Lisbon Lions, the club's 1967 European Cup winning team, in the 50th anniversary season of their triumph.

Brendan Rodgers would see it every time he stepped off the Celtic team bus to enter the stadium on match days. The manager never felt burdened by the history. Instead it inspired him.

He wanted his players to respond to the past in the same away. He asked them to embrace the club's standards and expectations, to respect Celtic's achievements and use this history to help create a successful future. Rodgers told them: Follow the star.

Jock Stein's Lions regularly featured in his team-talks over the course of the season, even though the world of football was unrecognisable from those halcyon days. In the modern era, Celtic could only dream of emulating the Lisbon Lions and becoming European champions. Yet there was nothing to stop them honouring the memory of Celtic's greatest-ever team through domestic dominance.

"The younger players can still be inspired by the Lions because the legend will never fade away," said Rodgers. "We are here because of them. They created the history. That's why when I first came in here I asked them to defend the culture of the club, which these guys created. The star at the top of the stadium is down to what they did in 1967.

"It was the same when I was at Liverpool. I was never frightened of the past as the great history was one of the big reasons I went there. At Melwood with Liverpool you used to walk in every morning and the European Cup was sat there. You walked past it and thought, 'I'd better be good today'.

"When you walk around Celtic Park, seeing the European Cup in the trophy cabinet as well, you say, 'Right, I'd better be good here'. Coming to Celtic I knew a lot more about the club as a supporter. That aspect was very strong in my thinking.

"We have to defend the traditions of Celtic as a club. It has always been an attacking club. You just have to go back to big Jock and what he created here. Our job is to entertain and win. My philosophy is non-negotiable. We attack."

'Pure, beautiful, inventive football' was how Stein described the Lions' style of play and Rodgers' aim was to create a modern-day Celtic team operating in the same traditions. During the closing minutes of a 5-2 win over St Johnstone on February 5, there was definitive proof that he'd succeeded. The hypnotic move started with a Nir Bitton tackle and ended with a typically calm Moussa Dembele finish. In between, 11 Celtic players were involved in a total of 25 passes. It was the goal of the season. In truth, it would have been the goal of any season.

Rodgers' improvement of the Celtic team he inherited from Ronny Deila had been evident long before full-back Mikael Lustig waltzed free inside the box and produced an extravagant rabona flick to help set up that goal in Perth. But in that moment at McDiarmid Park, it became abundantly clear just how monumental the transformation was.

Celtic were 2-1 behind at half-time as St Johnstone asked serious questions of them, but Rodgers' players came up with answers. Mentally, they remained strong and there was a sense of calm that hadn't always been evident in previous seasons. The Celtic players had total belief that they would work their way back into the game if they stuck to their principles, kept possession and probed for openings. St Johnstone had put in a power of work but Rodgers felt they would tire, and they did.

Dembele's introduction from the bench for the last half hour gave the home side a different problem. Celtic had a focal point now and the French striker swept in a penalty equaliser. It was a soft award but Rodgers' men were ruthless. Scott Sinclair and Dembele made it 4-2, before Celtic produced the PFA Scotland Goal of the Season to round off the win.

"I've never been part of a goal like that before," said Lustig. "Every player touched the ball before we scored and that shows how much confidence we have. My rabona wasn't disrespectful. It just felt right. When you have confidence in your game, you try things."

The goal had everything. Patience, skill, individual creativity and a killer finish. The fluidity of movement, which led to a right-back operating on the left edge of an opponent's penalty box, was exactly what Rodgers wanted from his Celtic team and hadn't happened by accident. It was the culmination of long hours spent on the training pitch.

The victory over St Johnstone took Celtic's unbeaten domestic run to 29 matches since the start of the season. A week previously, they had broken the 26-game record set by the Lisbon Lions in that historic 1966/67 season. Rodgers' team did it in style too, dismantling Hearts 4-0 at home.

Between September 18 and March 12, Celtic won a total of 28 domestic games in a row. This run was bookended by draws with Inverness Caledonian Thistle and Rangers but their consistency, given that the energy-sapping Champions League campaign lasted until December, was incredible.

Celtic needed to dig deep to get over the line in certain games. They cruised to victories most weeks at home but on away trips there were difficult obstacles and challenges put in their way. Yet whenever they were asked questions, Rodgers' players always seemed to come up with answers.

At Motherwell's Fir Park on December 3, Celtic trailed 2-0 at half-time as their unbeaten run looked to be coming at an end. Rodgers tweaked his system at the break, moving to a back three and pushing Callum McGregor, a first-half substitute for Emilio Izaguirre, into midfield.

The Celtic manager described it as a 3-4-3 formation

but it looked more like a 3-6-1 and the system seemed to spook Motherwell. There was no barrage of long balls or hopeful crosses from Celtic. Instead, they patiently kept possession, moved the play from side to side and simply waited for space to open up. Attacking midfielders McGregor, Stuart Armstrong and Tom Rogic positioned themselves behind Dembele, leaving him alone up front. This left the Motherwell defence with a major problem when wingers James Forrest and Patrick Roberts drifted infield.

Mark McGhee's back four were wary of being dragged out of position but were forced to step up and engage. It left them susceptible to being carved open and McGregor's goal to make it 2-1, a clinical 14-yard finish after a one-two with Armstrong, showed how effective this patient approach was for Celtic. "We found it a bit harder to cope," said Motherwell's Stephen McManus.

Roberts then equalised but Lionel Ainsworth's back-post volley put Motherwell ahead again, and tested the resolve of Rodgers' players once more. The response was instant. Roberts had the vision to pick out Armstrong's late run and the midfielder's touch and finish were perfect. Rogic's dancing feet then created space for an emphatic last-minute winner.

"We were absolutely brilliant second half," said Rodgers. "To score the four goals, to win the game, it really shows the mentality across the team. I have to give them huge credit because we had to put risk in the game. They took on the risk and they got the reward."

Celtic's growing mental strength was also evident on their next visit to Lanarkshire, on Christmas Eve. Hamilton Academical's artificial pitch can be a treacherous surface and McGregor's soft red card early in the second half posed an even more difficult challenge for Rodgers' team.

Leigh Griffiths' first-half goal had given Celtic the lead but Hamilton were now expected to press home the extra man advantage. Rodgers, though, had drilled his team for this situation and put his 10-man contingency plan into action. Instead of sending on an extra midfielder, he ordered Scott Sinclair to play higher up the pitch next to Dembele, who had replaced Griffiths at half-time.

Celtic adapted quickly to an unusual 4-3-2 formation, with both forwards occupying the Hamilton backline by constantly drifting wide in front of a narrow three-man midfield. It was a surprising tactical change but it worked. Hamilton never got to grips with Celtic's unconventional system and the game was comfortable as Armstrong and Dembele scored to seal a 3-0 win.

"Getting a man sent off presented us with a different challenge but we had prepared for that," said Rodgers. "We do a lot of work in training on overload, on ten versus nine, eight against seven.

"That was our first chance to look at it in a game and I was looking forward to that. We went to 4-3-2 so we can be attacking with two strikers up and we still have our three in midfield.

"There is not a lot of change, but there is a subtle difference. When we get to that final third we still looked really threatening and could have scored more than three. So it was a very good win at a notoriously difficult place."

A week later, Celtic were at Ibrox for their second Premiership meeting of the season with Rangers. It was New Year's Eve and the hosts were keen to end 2016 on a high. Protecting an unbeaten home record stretching back to September 2015, Mark Warburton's side started brightly and Rodgers' defence looked uneasy against the early onslaught.

Kenny Miller's opening goal gave Rangers belief but Celtic gradually grew into the game and Dembele's crashing left-foot volley restored parity before half-time. Celtic's performance levels improved dramatically after the interval and Sinclair's back-post finish put them ahead.

Miller hit the woodwork with a glaring chance on a late counter-attack but, overall, it was a merited three points for Rodgers' team in a convincing derby win.

"We talked before the game about what would happen if we fell behind, about dealing with pressure and finding solutions," said Rodgers. "The most pleasing thing is we stayed very calm and once we got the goal, we played our way back into the game again.

"We needed to adjust one or two things at half-time, but second half we were brilliant. We were a threat every time we went forward. We're disappointed to only get two goals. Scott Sinclair was incredible. For any player to play to that level in such a high-profile game was great."

An eventful 2016 had drawn to a successful close and the Celtic players scattered to all corners of the world on holiday. With the Premiership winter break now kicking in, it would be three weeks until they were back in competitive action, against Albion Rovers in the Scottish Cup.

Inside Ibrox on New Year's Eve, Rodgers told his squad to enjoy themselves and to be proud of what they had achieved in the first six months of the season. They were ordered to rest and recuperate, yet the hard work would soon start again. The Celtic manager had already set new goals for the remainder of the season.

Following a short break, the Celtic squad met up again in Dubai for a week of warm-weather training. With so many games in the first half of the season, Rodgers' in-depth tactical work had been limited. The hectic schedule meant players were constantly recovering but Dubai was a chance to get some sustained time on the training pitch with the full squad.

Refreshed after a week off, the Celtic squad trained hard during this period. They worked on base fitness and longer single sessions focused specifically on team-work and adding extra intensity to their collective ability to press opponents. "Going to Dubai was a chance to hit the reset button and the message has been very, very simple: we need more and we need to be better," said Rodgers.

"We've had a good period but we want more. We can defend better to allow us to attack more. So in Dubai we were talking about creating more pressure with speed, power and aggression in our game. We can create more chances through defending better in moments, as a collective."

Celtic, with Ivory Coast teenager Eboue Kouassi on board as the sole January signing from Russian club FC Krasnodar, returned from the winter break ready to meet the next set of challenges as they closed in on the Lions' unbeaten domestic record. On Sunday, January 29, they broke that long-standing run with a four-goal demolition of Hearts at Celtic Park.

Injuries to Dembele and Griffiths meant Rodgers was forced to field a team without a recognised striker. Yet the fitness, aggression and ability of his Celtic team meant that this wasn't even noticed. Roberts was asked to play as a 'false' No.9 and Hearts couldn't live with their opponents' movement and relentless pressing.

"They are out there on their own now, which is an incredible achievement," said Rodgers after creating the new 27-game unbeaten record. "It's huge. I know the history of this club and how difficult it is. So it's an incredible run and the idea now is to keep going. I've said to them we just have to keep winning and keep setting the bar higher."

Rodgers was back behind his desk at Lennoxtown the next morning, plotting a way to overcome Celtic's next challenge and setting fresh targets. Given that his team had just broken a proud record set by Stein's greats, it was fitting that he was able to celebrate the milestone with John Clark, the Lisbon Lion who continued to work as a kit co-ordinator at Celtic.

"When I sit with John and have a cup of tea after training or meet some of the other Lions, they give you little bits of gold dust," said Rodgers. "Not many people can do that.

"These were guys who weren't playing for the money. They were playing for the love of football and the love of Celtic. My job is to make sure we measure up to the standards these guys created, both on the pitch and in terms of humility. They are always at the forefront of everything we do."

CRAIG GORDON
OLD DOG, NEW TRICKS

CRAIG GORDON closed the door to Brendan Rodgers' Lennoxtown office and entered a dark place. It was Friday, August 26, and the Celtic goalkeeper should have been savouring Champions League qualification for the first time in his career. Instead, he was trying to process the news that he was no longer the club's first-choice No.1.

The Scotland international had saved a penalty in the European play-off win over Hapoel Be'er Sheva in Israel days earlier and was hailed as a hero. Yet within 72 hours, he was relegated to the bench as new signing Dorus de Vries assumed the role as Rodgers' chosen one.

Gordon was left bewildered. Then 33, the deposed Celtic goalkeeper would have been forgiven for seeking a transfer in the final days of the summer window. In England, there were several interested clubs just waiting for the signal.

De Vries had previously worked with Rodgers at

Swansea and arrived from Nottingham Forest with a ringing endorsement from the manager. Regarded as one of the British game's most accomplished 'sweeper keepers', the Dutchman appeared to be the final piece in Rodgers' Celtic jigsaw.

The outlook was bleak for Gordon. He had watched Manchester City's Joe Hart being dropped and sent out on loan to Torino for similar reasons. Pep Guardiola wanted a goalkeeper who was capable of pinging passes and catching crosses. Hart's status as England's No.1 didn't hold any weight as he packed his bags for Italy.

Gordon was in an eerily similar position and had a choice: request a transfer or work harder than ever to win back his place. Fuelled by anger and confusion, he admitted months later that he did initially fear his Celtic career was over.

"That was the obvious first reaction," he said. "Then after about two days I thought, 'Let's do something about it.'"

It took Gordon less than five games to win his place back. He replaced the injured De Vries at half-time against Kilmarnock on September 25 and stayed there for the rest of the season. By January, Celtic were knocking back bids of over £3million from Chelsea for the goalkeeper.

In March, Gordon was given a wage increase and signed a new contract until 2020. Days later, after an outstanding performance in a 1-1 Premiership draw against Rangers, Rodgers called him "one of the top goalkeepers in Europe".

It was a remarkable turnaround in the space of a few short months, yet nobody should be surprised that Gordon came back from the brink at Celtic.

Determination has never been something that the keeper has lacked.

Before joining Celtic in July 2014, Gordon had spent two years out of football through injury. His last competitive game for Sunderland was in April 2012 but by then he was already hampered by serious knee problems, having torn his patella tendon twice. He was freed weeks later and, crippled by pain, feared his career was over.

During the course of the next two years, Gordon came close to retiring as he struggled to regain full fitness. At one point, cashing in an insurance policy was an option. "To get the pay-out, I would have had to officially retire and not play any form of professional football," said Gordon. "It would have gone to a settlement and it was pretty close to getting the go-ahead."

Gordon never signed that form. Having already undergone three operations, he started to study alternative treatment. He travelled to Barcelona and London for courses of injections and then began working through a rehab programme with Rangers physio Steven Walker.

The goalkeeper gradually grew stronger, to the point where he was able to take part in three training sessions a week. Urged on by his family, Gordon wanted to give himself one last chance of reviving his top-level career. Celtic goalkeeping coach Stevie Woods invited him to take part in training sessions towards the end of season 2013/14 and he signed weeks later.

Financially, it was a contract that represented little risk for the club. Gordon was the one putting everything on the line. There was no guarantee he would even be capable of playing competitively over a prolonged period but he didn't want to retire wondering what might have been.

"I arrived as a training goalkeeper to see how it went, with no real expectation of how my injury or how my career would pan out from there," he said. "It was a little bit of a leap of faith to go and see if I could still cope with this level of football."

What happened next bordered on the miraculous. Celtic's first-choice goalkeeper Fraser Forster joined Southampton and suddenly Gordon was thrust into the front line again. From nowhere, he had a chance to resurrect his career at a huge club. Gordon didn't waste it.

His first season, 2014/15, saw him crowned Scotland's Player of the Year as Celtic won the Premiership title and League Cup. The next campaign wasn't as spectacular but he remained a senior figure in a championship-winning team and retained that status for the first two months of Rodgers' reign.

By late August 2016, however, all of his dedication and perseverance was worthless as Rodgers opted to make a change and install De Vries. Yet after the initial shock, Gordon refused to settle for being back-up goalkeeper. He had battled through too much adversity to simply accept that fate.

Gordon threw himself into the challenge of displacing De Vries. He spoke at length to Rodgers and Woods, about the new manager's demands for the position. The clear message was that Rodgers wanted goalkeepers to begin moves with measured passes, not give the ball away cheaply with safety-first clearances.

Possession is king in Rodgers' eyes. He demands that

goalkeepers retain the ball whenever possible, but he initially doubted whether Gordon could do that to the levels he wanted.

The most gifted Scottish goalkeeper of his generation, Gordon broke the British transfer record for a player in that position when Sunderland paid Hearts £9million to sign him in 2007. He was of the highest calibre but there was a general feeling within the game that kicking wasn't one of his strong points.

In hindsight, that was harsh. In Gordon's final domestic appearance before losing his place to De Vries, against St Johnstone, his pass completion rate was over 90% from 40 attempts. Yet Gordon was also quick to admit that Rodgers' dedication to playing out from the back was new to him.

At the goalkeeper's previous clubs, Hearts and Sunderland, a direct style of play led to him regularly aiming long kicks for target-men strikers like Mark De Vries and Kenwyne Jones. Back then, a goalkeeper's sole job was to keep the ball out of the net. Nobody ever analysed Gordon's pass completion stats when he was starting his career.

Rodgers' modern outlook led to different challenges for a goalkeeper but this wasn't something Gordon feared. He studied footage of his European peers to discover exactly what the Celtic manager required from him and gain a better understanding of where he would have to improve.

"The manager was trying to develop me as a player and make sure I knew what he was looking for if there was ever a time I came back into the team," said Gordon.

"We sat down and spoke about things, and Stevie Woods also looked out clips of other keepers across the world doing what the manager was looking for. It was a case of studying how they did it, what type of pass to make and in what stage of the game.

"Before Celtic I never played in a team where we had most of the possession and you're always looking to build from the back. That's not saying I wouldn't have been able to do it earlier on. I probably would have. I'm in my mid 30s now but that doesn't matter. You can still learn to do it."

Gordon's studious approach paid off. Within weeks of his return to the team, the Celtic goalkeeper appeared far more confident with the ball at his feet as he played inch-perfect passes out from the back. The old dog learned new tricks.

"Probably 90% of my touches now are with my feet," said Gordon. "When that happens, I need to make sure my touch is right and that I'm helping the team. In one game against Hamilton, I didn't make many saves but I came off feeling good because I'd passed the ball around well and put it in the areas we wanted to go and create attacks.

"That's part of my role now. It gives me great satisfaction coming off with a clean sheet and having contributed to the team more, in terms of passing the ball or keeping possession, than with my actual goalkeeping work."

Dens Park on March 19 was a perfect example of this. Stuart Armstrong's goal in the 2-1 win over Dundee came at the end of a flowing move, started off by Gordon. He exchanged short passes with Jozo Simunovic and then picked out full-back Mikael Lustig, who was intentionally standing close to the touchline, over 40 yards up the pitch.

That precise, lofted pass took out three Dundee players and Celtic made them pay. Moussa Dembele, Callum McGregor and James Forrest were all involved before Armstrong bulleted his header into the corner. The Celtic players embraced the scorer but the manager immediately turned to his goalkeeper and started applauding. "Craig's selection of pass was brilliant," said Rodgers.

Gordon, however, was also quick to point out the importance of the collective team effort in the development of his passing range. Rodgers and his coaching staff spent hours drilling players on which positions to take up when he received the ball in any given area inside the penalty box, in order to provide the goalkeeper with more options. It was all about movement and angles.

In general, the full-backs will position themselves high, allowing the centre halves to split. Celtic's deep-lying midfielder will then drop deep, with the central striker finding space further up the pitch. Gordon's accuracy was naturally important but his instant awareness of where team-mates would be allowed him to concentrate on finding those areas.

"The manager works with the team for them to make the angles, it's not all about a keeper playing it out from the back," said Gordon. "It's the options he has and the players knowing the movements and what to expect when the ball goes back.

"That takes a lot of time to get everyone on the same page. But by the time I came back into the team after being out, the groundwork had been done. Everyone else had started to realise what they had to do to make things easier.

"Now and again I take part in outfield training. When we're doing possession, I might join in, and when we're doing patterns of play, more often than not it starts from me. It's up to me to be in the right positions to start us off. I have to be an option. It is about forgetting where the goal is and just thinking about where the right angle is for the pass.

"If the pass is on and I get the ball then it doesn't matter where the goal is, because I am keeping the ball for the team. It's something that I've had to learn. It's okay saying you are going to play out from the back but there needs to be a system and people in the right places to receive the ball. We've worked hard on that, at least two days a week in training."

Gordon won Rodgers over quickly upon his return to the team and the Celtic manager admitted he had been too quick to drop him after the Be'er Sheva game.

"Craig and I had a really good chat when I was going to make the change of goalkeeper but Dorus was injured when he signed and maybe I pushed him in too early, to try and impose the way we want to work," he said.

"I take that responsibility. The good thing about Craig is he wasn't a senior player who went away and sulked. He wanted to be better and learn what I want from a keeper.

"I watched games previously when the ball would go back to Craig and you would hear the noise of the crowd. Now he's producing passing masterclasses from the back – playing in a way nobody thought he could.

"When I speak to managers after games, they all talk about how Craig is so good on the ball. They say, 'He's better than some of my centre-halves'. That's a player who last season was getting rid of the ball. Now he's passing it. There is a difference. He's a footballer, not a goalkeeper."

By January, it wasn't just Scottish Premiership managers who were casting admiring glances towards Gordon. Chelsea were in the market for a back-up goalkeeper to Thibaut Courtois and made two bids of over £3million for Gordon towards the end of the transfer window.

It would have been a financially lucrative deal for both Celtic and Gordon but, months after dropping him, Rodgers refused to even entertain talk of his first-choice goalkeeper being sold. Chelsea weren't deterred but were repeatedly told they were wasting their time.

By then, Gordon had also regained his status as Scotland's No.1 goalkeeper and with impressive Champions League performances behind him, the Celtic manager was adamant it was a move that made no sense for either party.

"It's been a long, hard road for Craig in the opening period here to get to the level where I wanted him to be," said Rodgers. "But he took it on board and trained hard and tactically he understood it. So I'm not really of the mindset to throw all of that out and be left having to look for another Champions League goalkeeper.

"Everyone can see Craig has gone to another level and has regained his international place. Chelsea is a fantastic club but for Craig it has to be about playing for as long as he can. This is the best place for him. He is enjoying it here but as a club we have to look after him as well."

Rodgers stuck to his word and lobbied for Gordon to get his deal. Little more than a month after the transfer window closed, Gordon signed the new, improved contract the manager had promised him in their lengthy chats during that period of Chelsea's interest.

The Celtic goalkeeper appreciated that support from his manager and as they shook hands on the deal inside that same office at Lennoxtown, the dark clouds of August had long since disappeared.

"It could have gone totally the opposite way and I could have been looking for a new club at the end of this season, rather than signing a new contract," said Gordon. "That's football, I suppose. You never know what is around the corner.

"But I did what I've always done when something has gone against me, I tried to figure out what I needed to do to overcome it. I did it that time I was out of the team and I'm sure there will be other challenges put in my way over the next three years, but I'm looking forward to overcoming them as well."

THE NEXT GENERATION

CELTIC'S full-time academy players gather together in the indoor hall at the Lennoxtown training ground. It is the first week of pre-season in late June and word has quickly spread that someone wants to talk to them.

A few moments later, the green swing door opens and in walks Brendan Rodgers. The wide-eyed teenagers in front of him immediately stand to attention. They are ready to take in every word from the new manager.

Rodgers smiles and introduces himself. "Where's young Jack?" he says, trying to pick out Jack Aitchison among the crowd of impressionable kids. A striker of major promise, he made history as Celtic's youngest ever scorer when he netted against Motherwell in the final game of the previous season, aged 16 years and 71 days. Aitchison identifies himself. "Well done," says Rodgers. "Congratulations on your goal."

The new Celtic manager addresses the kids for a while

longer, assuring them that they will get chances under him if they work hard. Then he departs, off to focus on important first-team matters. Yet Rodgers was always there in the background, constantly assessing Celtic's promising batch of youngsters and playing a significant, influential role in their development.

Some managers pay little attention to what's happening in their club's academy, but Rodgers is different. He has a long background in youth development at Reading and Chelsea and knows how important it is. Celtic had always reared their own and Rodgers vowed to continue that tradition when he accepted the job.

Rodgers wasn't just at Celtic to win trophies and enhance his reputation. First-team matters remained the priority but as the events of his first season showed, the manager also felt an obligation to guide the next generation.

This was why, as he approached his 100th day at Celtic in late August, he rejected the chance to take a holiday in order to spend more time with the club's academy staff. Rodgers called an in-service day on August 31, with coaches congregating at Lennoxtown to learn more about his 'One Vision, One Club' philosophy.

The Celtic manager spoke about his admiration for the work carried out by Chris McCart, the Head of Youth, and his staff. The presence of Kieran Tierney, James Forrest, Liam Henderson and Callum McGregor as mainstays of his first-team squad was proof that the academy was producing talent.

Over the course of the season, he blooded several more. Aitchison, Calvin Miller, Anthony Ralston and Mikey Johnston were all rewarded with games at various points of the season. The latter two both excelled in their first starts in the 4-1 win over St Johnstone in May, and afterwards Rodgers made a point of raising their arms aloft as they took the acclaim of the Celtic fans.

Rodgers always looks within for talent and saw it as his duty to ensure the culture he was creating at the highest level within the club was passed down and shared throughout the age groups. He demanded that every coach and player, at every level, be made aware of the standards he set and expected to be maintained.

The manager was generous with his time. He delivered another presentation to coaches and teachers at St Ninian's High in Kirkintilloch in September, where Celtic run a successful school programme for elite youngsters.

Set up in 2008, the system was the first of its kind in Scotland and is designed to give Celtic's most talented young players extra coaching time before and after school. They report around 7am, train at St Ninian's pitches and go to school there, before being bussed to Celtic's training base at Lennoxtown after classes for more sessions.

Tierney is the poster boy of that venture and Rodgers could see the value in ensuring the club's best kids were getting a top-quality football and academic education.

He had worked with the elite in England. He knew what it took for a young player to reach the very top and was always quick to remind the club's young players that dedication to their profession was essential.

They all had talent, otherwise they wouldn't be at Celtic. But were they devoted to the game? Were they willing to make the required sacrifices to become Champions League players?

Overall, Rodgers maintained more of a watching

brief with the younger players, allowing McCart and professional academy coach Tommy McIntyre to get on with their jobs, but there was still regular interaction. Rodgers took every opportunity to tell and even show these kids what it would take to make it at Celtic as a first-team player.

One December afternoon, Rodgers was walking down the first-floor corridor at Lennoxtown when he glanced inside the gym and noticed a figure in the corner, carrying out an intense stretching workout. It was Kolo Toure. The Ivorian was rarely featuring at that point of the season and was heading towards the end of an illustrious career.

Yet Toure, then 35, was still willing to put the hours in. This work ethic was why he had a long, decorated period at the highest level in England. It was the reason he became an Arsenal Invincible.

Rodgers regarded him as the perfect role model and felt this little snapshot was too good an opportunity to miss. He had to share it with those players sitting inside the youth canteen.

"I went to the under-20s and interrupted their lunch, which I apologised for," he said, recalling the Toure episode. "I said, 'Sorry guys, come with me a second' and I took them into the gym.

"Kolo was in there doing his activation, stretching... at 35 years of age. He could have been away home, but a few hours after he'd finished training he was in the gym on his own.

"That's what you need to do to be a top player. It doesn't start when you arrive at the training ground, it starts with your first waking moment. Then when you drive out, it doesn't end. It's a lifestyle. It's right the way through. Body mass, body fat, you need to look after it all. The guys who will play on until they're 35 are the ones who have been looking after their body. If you have a brain to add to your brawn, then you'll have a chance.

"The key thing is not the young boys' talent. It's whether they want to devote their life to it. If you want to operate at the level of Champions League, be a world-class player or the very best player you can be, you have to develop technically, tactically, socially, and in terms of your lifestyle."

In truth, lifestyle was shorthand for diet. Were Celtic's young players willing to stay clear of alcohol and takeaways? Were they prepared to fuel their bodies in the proper way, at the right time? Did they get the required amount of rest before training and games?

Rodgers was willing to disclose that he had some doubts on this front with regards to one of Celtic's most talented starlets. But if tough love was required, he was prepared to provide it.

"I have witnessed one or two up here with big talents but when it gets tough they go the other way," said Rodgers. "This is key. They need to understand that if you want to be a Champions League player, or be the best you can be, your talent is not enough. You need to prepare in every facet of your life to be a player.

"There is talent here in Scotland, no question about that. There are players with ability and they have every opportunity now to be a footballer. Are they going to take it? Or are they, when it gets a wee bit tough, going to look for the easy way? Do they eat the right things? Do they lead the life of a footballer? That is the main thing.

"I've had one player in here and I hope he sees the light, as he's a massive talent. He could play Champions

League football. He had all the tools but he was fat. Couldn't run. Couldn't last a game. Not eating right. Fish and chips all the time.

"We organised a plan for him, to sort him out, if he wants to do it. But I don't worry about it. It doesn't break my heart because some other kid with less talent but who commits to it, will make a player. The key thing is not if the boy is a talent, it is whether they want to devote their life to it.

"I've spoken to enough players in my career who blame everyone else. They blame the coach, they blame never getting the chance. They don't take responsibility. It's everyone else's fault.

"This is where I have been very clear with the Celtic kids from 16s to 20s. I tell them, 'You have opportunities here, with some of the best facilities in the country, at one of the biggest clubs in the world. You have every tool here in order to be the best player. You need to commit to it. We will have a plan for you to get into the first team, but the crown is on your head'.

"I've told them, 'Stop taking short-cuts, stop blaming everyone else and get on with being an elite player. And if you just fall short of an excellent level, you'll still have a career.'"

Rodgers' words on diet and lifestyle had an impact on Celtic's academy players. Aitchison disclosed how he'd even been inspired to give up his one guilty pleasure of Nutella chocolate spread. "I used to have the odd cheat day but I'll maybe have something once a month now, at the most," he said.

The Celtic manager viewed the period from 16 to 20 years as defining for any player. Learning the right habits and sticking to them was crucial if they were to become

Champions League players. Below that, in the Junior and Intermediate sections of Celtic's three-tier academy structure, he was happy to let the younger kids develop with more freedom, while still being given essential basic guidance on diet and lifestyle.

Yet he remained aware of everything that was going on at the club and took a hands-on role in the unique case of Karamoko Dembele, a 14-year-old Celtic player. Of Ivory Coast origin, he was born in London and raised in Glasgow, and was a superstar in the making.

The diminutive left-footed attacker had created a buzz with his virtuoso performances in the lower age groups. Playing against opponents almost twice his size, he simply glided past them with a mixture of pace, skill and balance.

Dembele's YouTube showreels from youth tournaments had been watched thousands of times and every major club in Europe, from Barcelona to Manchester United, coveted his signature. The comparisons to Lionel Messi were immediate and understandable.

With growing interest from across the world, the Celtic manager met his family early in his tenure and invited young Karamoko to take part in a light, technical session with the senior players at Lennoxtown. This involvement highlighted the regard in which the club held the player but Rodgers was also determined not to push Dembele too far, too soon, at such a young age. Yet this didn't all go to plan initially.

What should have been a low-key Scottish Development League under-20 game between Celtic and Hearts at Cappielow on October 3 suddenly captured the attention of football fans across Europe. Aged just

13 at that point, Dembele was named among the Celtic substitutes and came on for the last nine minutes in a 3-1 win. The reaction was instant and the hype spiralled out of control.

For days, it seemed like Karamoko Dembele was the name on everyone's lips. His outing had taken place during the second international break of the season and the lack of top-level domestic football only heightened the coverage. "I'm convinced when Karamoko was born he immediately nutmegged the midwife," was the reaction from one of Dembele's first boys' club coaches.

Rodgers, though, refused to contribute to the circus. He was out of the country on a break when Dembele made his under-20 debut and hadn't been made aware it was happening. When the Celtic manager finally had his say, some 10 days later, he made it clear that he wasn't comfortable with the level of exposure.

In a pointed appeal for calm, Rodgers also warned of the potential pitfalls for a player of his age as he vowed to take full control of his development from that moment on. That would be Dembele's first and last under-20 appearance of the season.

"I didn't know he was playing," said Rodgers. "Would I have sanctioned it? That's not the point. The point is he's played. In the modern world, everything is a story. You just have to be very careful. He is a child, he's a baby. He's a talented boy at 13 years of age and has had a lot of attention.

"He's not a 13-year-old in the body of a 19-year-old. He doesn't have those maturation levels. He really looks 13. As much as what his ability is and how fast he is, the worry for me when I saw it was 'What if a 25-year-old

Brendan Rodgers and Lisbon Lion John Clark toast Celtic's record of 27 domestic games unbeaten from the start of the season. The previous record had been set by Jock Stein's European Cup-winning team in 1966/67

Craig Gordon celebrates signing his new Celtic contract on March 8 after the club rebuffed interest from Chelsea in the January transfer window

Celtic players celebrate on the Ibrox pitch after the 5-1 win over Rangers on April 29. Celtic dominated the derby from start to finish with a devastating attacking display

Brendan Rodgers is joined by his backroom staff after agreeing a new four-year contract.
Left to right: first-team coach John Kennedy, head of performance Glen Driscoll, assistant Chris Davies and goalkeeping coach Stevie Woods

Brendan Rodgers leads youth academy graduates Mikey Johnston and Anthony Ralston towards the fans after the 4-1 win over St Johnstone on May 6. Both impressed on their first competitive starts

Celtic fans unveil a spectacular tifo paying tribute to the Lisbon Lions' 1967 European Cup win before the last Premiership game of the season against Hearts on May 21

Scott Brown holds aloft the Scottish Premiership trophy as Celtic celebrate becoming the Invincibles and securing a sixth successive title win

A clean sweep at the PFA Scotland awards. Brendan Rodgers was named Manager of the Year, Scott Sinclair was Player of the Year, Kieran Tierney was Young Player of the Year and Moussa Dembele claimed the Goal of the Season award

The goal that clinched an Invincible Treble. Helpless Aberdeen players look on as Tom Rogic squeezes an injury-time shot past Joe Lewis to win the Scottish Cup for Celtic at Hampden

Tom Rogic runs towards the Celtic supporters after scoring an injury-time Scottish Cup final winner against Aberdeen

Celtic's Invincibles celebrate the last part of the Treble as Scott Brown holds aloft the Scottish Cup. Brendan Rodgers urged every member of the playing squad and backroom staff to gather on the podium for the historic moment

Brendan Rodgers savours a perfect first season at Celtic as he shows off the Scottish Cup to the supporters

An emotional Kieran Tierney grabs the Celtic badge on his jersey as he lifts the Scottish Cup. The teenager was taken off with a serious mouth injury during the final and raced through departing Aberdeen fans on foot to return to Hampden in time for the presentation

Brendan Rodgers poses
with the three trophies –
the league, League Cup and
Scottish Cup – he won in
his record-breaking first
season at Celtic

tackles him'. I'm a father and as good as they are, I worry from a parent's perspective. But he's a talent and it will be managed going forward. Will I take a more hands-on role? Yes.

"I took him in for one session early on in my time here as when I arrived I'd heard about his talent, but he just needs to be left alone to develop. Then hopefully he can go and achieve, and make the steps we want him to.

"Karamoko is young and there is so much development and so much needs to happen for him to go on and become a player. At this moment in time, he's a big talent, we have to nurture it and ensure he is challenged – at the right times.

"The guys who work in the Celtic academy are very good at their job. I trust them and it's not an issue. I'm sure they probably never realised the scope of media attention it would have had. But it's football, I oversee football."

Rodgers took this remit seriously throughout the season. In the days leading up to Celtic's final two Premiership games against Partick Thistle and Hearts, he found time in a hectic schedule to spend an evening at Barrowfield, the training ground used by the Lisbon Lions and Martin O'Neill's Celtic team, watching Junior Academy sessions involving kids aged between eight and 12.

The visit was part of his vision for a one-club philosophy from the bottom all the way up to the first team and it showed Celtic's academy coaches that Rodgers was committed to taking an interest in every level. "I was an under-10 coach once and if the first-team manager acknowledged them it meant everything," said

Rodgers. "However long I'm here I want to influence the club in the most positive way possible."

Invincible

KIERAN TIERNEY
FROM BALLBOY TO TOP BHOY

"What I love about Kieran is that every pass he makes
is for Celtic. Every header he makes is for Celtic.
Every tackle is for Celtic. Kieran would be in the stand
if he wasn't playing. He absolutely loves the club."
Brendan Rodgers, October 3, 2016

AIKENHEAD Road, Glasgow. May 27, 2017. The
digital clock on the dashboard shows 5.08pm as the
car carrying Kieran Tierney attempts to turn right into
the Hampden car park.

The Celtic full-back is in a race against time. His
Scottish Cup final ended prematurely 90 minutes earlier,
when he was floored by a swinging elbow from Jayden
Stockley, the Aberdeen striker. He has undergone
emergency dental treatment to fix shattered teeth and a
damaged jaw five miles away in Govan. He is now on his
way back. The strong painkillers have kicked in by the

time the stadium comes into view. Tierney is desperate to be inside, joining in Celtic's Treble celebrations. Scott Brown is about to climb those famous Hampden steps to lift the trophy but the teenager is stuck outside. His vehicle is blocked from entering the car park. With Aberdeen fans departing in their thousands, there is no way through.

The teenager weighs up his options. The car door flies open and he begins to run towards the stadium, through hordes of supporters. Still dressed in his Celtic kit, Tierney's studs clatter off the road as he reaches the stairs leading to the Hampden reception area. He bounds up them two at a time and goes through the front door.

At that moment, the Celtic end erupts as Brown lifts the Scottish Cup. Tierney hears the roar as he dashes downstairs and eventually makes it to the tunnel area. From there, he walks up the steps to join his team-mates, where he is the last player to be presented with a medal. Moussa Dembele embraces him and passes the trophy.

An iconic image follows. Already a hero to the Celtic fans, Tierney completely lets go of his emotions. Pumping the badge on his strip, he roars towards the fans who idolise him. The pain from his injury momentarily subsides, replaced by sheer euphoria.

He is a Celtic Invincible and a Treble winner.

THIS is what Tierney dreamed about a year earlier when he began preparing for the new season. He could have headed to Mexico or Ibiza with dozens of other young footballers for a party that summer. Instead, he hired a personal trainer.

The Celtic left-back knew how big season 2016/17 would be for him. He had listened to all the warnings after an impressive breakthrough campaign. Aged 19, Tierney realised he was under considerable pressure to maintain his progress after Brendan Rodgers' arrival and keep the experienced Emilio Izaguirre out of the team.

"People asked me if I was scared of second-season syndrome," said Tierney. "It has happened to players before but you try to blank that sort of thing out. If you think about that too much, the mental side will get to you."

Tierney instead approached the new season with a clear mind and positive outlook. There had been no secret to his success up to that point. It was down to the right attitude and a willingness to work hard. Other players his age might have allowed the adulation and money to go to their heads. Tierney just resolved to put in more sweat and toil than ever before during the summer of 2016.

He spent 10 days relaxing in the Canary Islands, travelled to the Isle of Man, his place of birth, to watch a motorcycle event and then focused on football. While his peers were pouring Grey Goose vodkas at pool parties, Tierney was doing two weeks of extra conditioning work with Mark Dickson, a private fitness coach.

When Tierney reported for the first day of pre-season training under Rodgers he looked fitter, faster and stronger. His upper body had bulked up in the close season. The stamina issues that had caused him problems in his early first-team outings were now firmly consigned to the past. Over the course of an outstanding season, he blossomed with every passing month.

Tierney's performances in 2015/16 under Ronny Deila earned him three Young Player of the Year awards, from Celtic, the Scottish PFA and the Scottish Football Writers Association. Just 12 months later, he made history by again picking up that trio of individual awards for his role in Celtic's dominant season. The hard work over the summer had paid off.

Rodgers knew all about Tierney prior to his arrival at Celtic. In the games he watched live on television, the left-back's aggression and ability stood out. John Collins, Deila's assistant, also gave the teenager a glowing reference during a conversation with the new manager. Rodgers was told Celtic had a gem on their hands and it didn't take him long to understand the hype.

"I saw in the first two days I was in charge that Kieran will be a top player," said Rodgers. "I know from my experience of working in England in the middle section and at the top end of the league, that this kid absolutely 100 per cent will be that.

"Having worked with young players and seen them grow and develop into top stars, there's no question about it. What stands out about him? Just about everything.

"He has the right attitude and he's quicker than I thought. I had only seen him in highlights and clips before coming here, but when you see him close up, he's a super athlete. He's strong, quick, balanced and aggressive. He has a wonderful left foot and will get better. Kieran defends well, he's hard to beat, he is a good size and he has personality."

One of Rodgers' first acts as Celtic manager was to sanction a new, improved five-year contract for him. It was the second extension he had been awarded in the space of 10 months but Celtic realised they had to protect a prized asset. Born in Douglas, on the Isle of Man, Tierney was raised in the Muirhouse area of Motherwell. His Celtic story began there at the age of seven. John McStay, father of former Celtic captain Paul, scouted Netherton Boys Club and spotted his talent. The invitation to training arrived shortly afterwards. Playing for Celtic was Tierney's dream. Michael, his father, had taken him to games from his earliest days. There is television footage of him being interviewed with a 12-year-old Kieran outside Hampden after Celtic's 2-0 Scottish Cup semi-final defeat by Ross County in 2010. "This is the future in front of us," says Michael, pointing to his son. It was a prophetic statement.

Tierney had a season ticket from a young age and idolised Bobo Balde, the powerful Guinean central defender of Martin O'Neill's all-conquering Celtic team of the early 2000s. Later on, Izaguirre became the player he looked up to.

"When you are younger, some people dream about playing in the English Premier League, I only dreamed about playing for Celtic," said Tierney. "It was always a Celtic strip I wore."

Martin Miller, head of Celtic's Junior Academy, had dozens of hopeful kids training at Barrowfield when Tierney arrived, but the tenacious left-sided kid stood out and officially signed for the club when he was at primary school. His progress continued and he was eventually offered a place at Celtic's school partnership with St Ninian's High in Kirkintilloch.

For Tierney, this meant extra travelling and long days. There were no guarantees that a professional contract would be offered at the end, either. When Tierney was approaching his 16th birthday he had to remain patient as Celtic's academy staff considered whether to offer him a full-time deal. He was one of the last to be signed up but it proved to be a wise decision. Tierney is now the poster boy for the St Ninian's system.

Just a year after he turned professional, with Ronny Deila appointed as manager, Tierney began to make inroads at a higher level. He was handed his first-team debut against Tottenham Hotspur in a 6-1 friendly defeat in August 2014 but really made an impression playing in a Celtic XI in Villarreal a month later. Up against far more experienced players, he looked comfortable.

Collins was in charge for that Spanish trip and made a bold prediction about what "little Kieran" would achieve in football after a 4-2 loss. "Kieran's passing was excellent. It was a wonderful performance from a kid who will go to the very top," said the Celtic assistant manager, inside El Madrigal's deserted media room.

Afterwards, Collins phoned Deila to fill him in on the performance, and reserved special praise for Tierney. It wasn't a full strength Villarreal team but the teenager excelled. This didn't surprise the Norwegian. "I saw that Kieran was a good player from the very first day I watched him," said Deila. "He is a big talent, who can operate at the highest level."

At that point in Tierney's career, a competitive debut seemed inevitable. He was named on the bench for the Premiership game against Ross County on December 27, 2014, but broke his leg in training 24 hours later, twisting it in a freak accident. "I was due to go to Gran Canaria with the first team in January, so it was hard to take. I ended up in a moon boot at New Year."

It was a crushing blow for the teenager but Deila and Collins promised him his chance before the end of the season. They monitored his rehabilitation closely and after Tierney returned to fitness, he made his league debut against Dundee in April 2015. Two months later, he signed a new four-year contract.

With Izaguirre established as Celtic's left-back, Tierney continued to serve his apprenticeship. Tyler Blackett also arrived on loan from Manchester United to compete in that area and Tierney made fleeting appearances. Yet his performance levels in training were of such a high standard that it was becoming harder for Deila to leave him out.

By October 2015, the Celtic manager realised he couldn't hold him back any longer. With Izaguirre serving a suspension, Tierney started ahead of Blackett against Fenerbahce in the Europa League. It was a big moment and he barely missed a game after that. He finished 2015/16 as an automatic choice and fans' favourite, with his own chant.

This meteoric rise led to his improved contract and the collection of every Young Player of the Year award available. The Scotland manager, Gordon Strachan, was also impressed and fast-tracked Tierney through the age groups to give him a first senior cap against Denmark in March 2016.

Defensively, there was nobody better in Scottish football. Strachan publicly declared Tierney to be the best "one on one" defender at Celtic and very few wingers got the better of a player known for his tenacity. It was for this reason that the Scotland manager felt confident enough to field him at right-back in a crucial World Cup qualifying win over Slovenia. His accomplished performance that night didn't come as a surprise to former Celtic manager Deila. The Norwegian takes great satisfaction from Tierney's progression and classes him as a rare breed of modern full-back, one who can defend and attack with equal ability.

"Kieran is gifted in terms of fitness, speed and agility," said Deila. "He is also tight defensively. We always get full-backs now who are very good offensively, but a lot of them lack defensive ability. When you are a full-back, first of all you are a defender. That's what KT is.

"He very rarely gets caught out of position, his eyes and ears are open all the time, and he hates losing tackles. At 18, he thought and played like a 25-year-old. KT has incredible ability."

What Rodgers brought to Tierney's game was more composure, especially in an attacking sense. The Celtic manager believed his partnership with Scott Sinclair on the left flank would be crucial to the dynamic of his team. The duo staged a daily darts game at Lennoxtown and a blossoming friendship transferred onto the pitch.

"We know each other's games inside out," said Sinclair at the midway point of the season. "KT's a great young player. He's getting tons of experience and he's a guy who wants to learn and gives 100 per cent, even in training. That's great to see."

Stuart Armstrong's goal against Rangers in the 5-1 derby victory in September showed how effective the Tierney/Sinclair axis could be. The left-back picked up possession on the halfway line, shifted the ball to the winger and immediately sprinted for the return beyond the Rangers full-back. Sinclair's weight of pass was perfect and Tierney had the vision to pick out Armstrong with a cutback. Rodgers developed the attacking part of Tierney's game to add extra quality in the final third, urging him to take a split-second before delivering his final ball. The teenager's two assists against Manchester City in the 3-3 Champions League draw was proof that this was paying off. Tierney claimed Celtic's second of the night, although it was credited as a Raheem Sterling own goal. Yet it was down to his desire to get forward on the left wing and his intelligence to smash the ball across the face of goal, forcing Sterling to deflect it in. For Celtic's third, Tierney had more time to deliver and the whip on his cross forced Aleksandar Kolarov into a mistake, allowing Moussa Dembele to score.

The City game was Tierney's first taste of a Champions League night on the Celtic Park pitch. He had been to many as a fan and was even closer to the action as a ballboy when Celtic famously humbled Barcelona in November 2012. "Victor Wanyama scored and ran towards me before checking away at the last minute," said Tierney. "Who would have known that the ballboy sitting in front of the Green Brigade would play for Celtic in the Champions League? It's madness."

In Celtic's 4-0 win over Hearts in late January, Tierney also produced a crossing masterclass that belonged at the highest level. It was the variety of his delivery that stood out most. One curling, dipping cross, after winning a crunching 50/50 tackle, should have been converted by Sinclair and earned the full-back a standing ovation.

The winger made no mistake after Tierney then hammered the ball across goal in Celtic's next attack. His cross was delivered with the ferocity of a shot and Sinclair pounced after Hearts failed to clear. For Celtic's fourth goal, Tierney then showed awareness to disguise his perfect cutback for Patrick Roberts. His man-of-the-match performance at Celtic Park that day was all the more remarkable, given that he had only returned to the team after undergoing two operations, on his ankle and shoulder. Those injuries led to a three-month absence, with Tierney missing the end of Celtic's Champions League campaign and the Betfred Cup final win over Aberdeen.

Yet he used that time wisely. "When you get injured, people think about the negatives and how long you will be out for," said Tierney. "I had to look the opposite way and think, 'Right, I can do these things to improve'. You have to think positive and I have a great team around me with family and sports scientists and physios. I did a lot of upper body strength and power to get more physical."

Tierney also saw that lay-off as an opportunity to go back to his roots and become a supporter again, joining his friends and family at Celtic away games. From Fir Park to Ibrox, he never missed a fixture. Tierney was mobbed on his way into away grounds by the fans who idolised him, but happily posed for photographs before cheering on Celtic like everyone else. "I loved it," he said. "I still feel like a fan. I still go mad when we score."

This summed up Tierney's refreshing outlook on his life and football career. Polite and modest, he doesn't view himself as a superstar. He is tied down on a lucrative contract at Celtic but continues to live with his parents. He is tee-total and is happier watching UFC and playing PlayStation games with his friends than going to nightclubs.

"I don't drink so when I'm out with my friends, we play pool, listen to music and just do normal stuff," said Tierney, who toasted Celtic's title win with a Diet Coke.

Invincible

"I have just never fancied alcohol. I don't know what will happen down the line, but I probably won't drink.

"It helps me as a footballer and I can't see me doing it any time soon. I celebrated my first title at Celtic with a Chinese meal. I do probably have to do different things to my friends at times, but that's been the same all my life.

"I knew at 13 I couldn't do some things because it would affect Celtic and that's the club I always wanted to play with. I have always been cautious. My friends realise that and that it's in my best interests. I made sacrifices when I was younger. My mum and dad told me that's what I had to do. It's paid off."

Tierney can also regularly be seen at the side of public parks across Lanarkshire supporting The Bullfrog FC. His friends play for the Sunday League team and the Celtic player made a low-key financial contribution towards their kit and equipment. Had his career gone in a different path, he would have been out there playing for The Bullfrog too.

Current Celtic captain Scott Brown believes Tierney will inherit his armband one day. "KT is a natural leader and a die-hard Celtic fan," he said. "He would be the one for me."

Those words meant a lot to Tierney, who views Brown as a mentor. The Celtic midfielder helped coach the club's under-20 team when the full-back was breaking through and Tierney will never forget the way Brown supported him after his leg break in December 2014.

"Scott and Craig Gordon were the first two players I heard from," said Tierney. "They wouldn't even have had my number, so the fact they went out of their way to get it tells you what kind of people they are. Broony is a legend here. He makes everyone feel welcome."

Future captain or not, Tierney feels privileged to be playing for Celtic. It didn't come easy for him either. There were moments in his academy years when he feared no professional contract would be coming. Those three operations in two years also tested his mental strength, but he bounced back stronger each time.

"Kieran is living the dream, a kid who has come through the system at Celtic and got a chance," said Rodgers. "He had a trauma here with the injury early on. To then come back from that shows the character he has. I always look at the young players who have had the little traumas in their life. The ones who have come through them tend to kick on. There is something in that adverse moment that can make you."

Invincible

LENNOXTOWN
A DAY IN THE LIFE

KOLO TOURE is shadow boxing as he jogs to the side of a training pitch at Lennoxtown. The Celtic defender throws an uppercut followed by a jab, just as Scott Sinclair starts darting in and out of luminous yellow poles with a ball at his feet.

Beyond them, up towards the back of the vast expanse of green turf, Moussa Dembele is curling free-kicks over four mannequins, honing his technique. At the same time, the touch and concentration levels of Celtic's central defenders are tested by the awkward bouncing balls thrown in their direction by coaching staff. Kieran Tierney is also there, working diligently on his weaker right foot.

In the middle of all this activity, Brendan Rodgers stands still, cradling a clipboard. He has just completed an intense 90-minute session with his entire first-team squad and looks on approvingly as players now go through their individually tailored drills. It's an impressive sight, even more so when you consider the date: April 13, 2017. Celtic are already Premiership champions for a sixth successive time. They are heading towards the end of a season that has already brought Champions League qualification and the Betfred Cup. Rodgers' debut campaign has been an unqualified success.

Yet there is always more work to be done. The Scottish Cup remains a target and Rodgers won't allow standards to drop. That was what he told his Celtic squad on their very first day of pre-season training on June 20, 2016.

It's after 12.30pm when Rodgers walks off the training pitch. By then, he has been at Lennoxtown for at least five hours already. It isn't unusual for him to stay at Celtic's training base well into the evening.

"I've always devoted my life to my career and my work," he said. "People who know me understand that's what drives me. I am a professional and this is my profession. I'm not here to take short cuts and get out to a golf course. I get paid a good salary by the club and I need to earn that."

Rodgers' late parents, Malachy and Christina, instilled this relentless work ethic in their son, the eldest of five boys. When injury ended his playing career at 20, he took up a full-time job at the John Lewis warehouse in Bracknell. He worked four 12-hour shifts every week, from 6am to 6pm. Then at night, he pursued his coaching career. "That was my time in the real world, when I learned about life," Rodgers said.

Under the Rodgers regime, Lennoxtown usually comes to life around 7am. The green iron gates to the training ground constantly slide open as Celtic's coaching and medical staff report for duty. Set against a picturesque backdrop of the Campsie hills in East Dunbartonshire, 14 miles from Celtic Park, the training ground sits in the shadow of the old Lennox Castle hospital. The £8million facility was opened in October 2007 and boasts four full-size pitches, one artificial surface and a small indoor hall.

First-team squad members are normally obliged to be on site for 9.30am but by then, hours of planning have been put in for the day ahead. Every session is structured and mapped out from start to finish.

Celtic use a periodised training programme to ensure players reach optimum physical condition for games. Sessions are always planned with this in mind. If Celtic are in the middle of a heavy run of fixtures, training will be more recovery-based and focused on technical aspects of performance.

In free midweeks, there is greater scope for tougher conditioning sessions in the early part of the week, before reducing the workload in the days before the weekend game. A balance is sought between the elite levels of fitness demanded by the manager, and the avoidance of fatigue before matchdays.

Rodgers and his assistants, Chris Davies and John Kennedy, work out a specific training plan for every day. Training sessions generally last between 60 and 90 minutes. The content varies, depending on what areas and themes Rodgers is keen to work on that day.

From defensive and offensive transitions to switching play and shape work, the Celtic manager has an array of drills developed over 20-plus years of coaching, to ensure a stimulating variety of work for his players. "It is not just a case of turning up, having a game of five-a-sides and being finished by 12 o'clock," said captain Scott Brown. "It's non-stop and you are learning all the time."

Rodgers constantly gives his players challenges during sessions. He will play games of 9 v 10 and drill them on coping with a man disadvantage. This work paid off throughout the season. Against Rangers in the Scottish Cup semi-final, Celtic were down to 10 men for over five minutes after Dembele limped off and Leigh Griffiths waited to come on. Yet the players didn't panic. The training-ground contingency plan kicked in and they slotted into a 4-4-1 shape to consolidate for that spell.

The Celtic manager hosts a training meeting at around 9am every day with all coaches and several members of the medical staff. The objectives of the session are explained and updates on any players' injuries are also delivered. Prior to seeing Rodgers, head of performance Glen Driscoll and his sports science and medical team have an 8.30am meeting to discuss player availability and any other issues.

By the time the training meeting is complete, the players have arrived at Lennoxtown. Jack Nayler, Celtic's head of sports science, speaks to the squad individually to gauge every player's condition. Any fresh ailments or injuries are reported at this stage. Even if someone has had a poor night's sleep, he is encouraged to disclose this information as state of mind can have an impact on performance levels.

Players eat breakfast in the dining room on the first floor at Lennoxtown. Everything is freshly prepared and of the highest quality, from fruit and vegetables to eggs. The players also carry out their own prehab work in the gym down the corridor, performing stretches or going through a light warm-up to avoid any muscular injuries.

Some prefer to have a massage before training begins at 10.30am. Rodgers' session on April 14 – part of an open training day at Celtic Park during the Easter Holidays – showcased the kind of high-tempo, sharp workout he favours in the days leading up to a game. It took place 48 hours before Celtic played Ross County away in a Premiership match and the intensity level was guided by the periodisation programme.

In that part of April, Celtic had seven clear days between fixtures. They had played on Saturday against Kilmarnock and the County game took place on the following Sunday. In the early days of that week, players recovered but the physical demands then increased towards the middle of the week before a light, technical session 24 hours prior to the game.

The Friday open session at Celtic Park began with a 10-minute warm-up, without the ball. Led by John Currie, Celtic's first-team sports scientist, the outfield players embarked on a lap of the pitch at a gentle pace and then went through a stretching routine. Short runs and more stretches followed, before some sharper footwork and five-yard sprints.

After a quick break for an energy drink or water, the players split into two groups for a couple of sharp drills. Four poles made out a square area and two different passing routines were completed during a five-minute spell. Players used alternate feet, aiming for crisp passing and instant control. At the same time, Celtic's goalkeepers performed their own warm-up.

With everyone warm and loosened off, Rodgers called his squad together for the first of the three main parts of the session. It was a 10 v 10 possession-based match on a condensed pitch, around 60 yards long and using the width of the 18-yard box. As the weekend fixture draws closer, Celtic shorten the pitch for training games of this nature to decrease the loading on the players.

Two mini goals were placed at each end and goalkeepers operated in the space between them, but only with their feet. The teams had been picked before the session, with yellow and orange bibs handed out during the warm-up.

The 15-minute game was played at high intensity. Players worked in their normal positions and shape, and were encouraged to play two-touch football. Each team got a point for scoring into one of the small goals or for making a run beyond the goalline to receive a pass.

There was little space on the pitch but the tight area was designed to work on players' pressing, touch and awareness. Goalkeepers were urged to pass out and keep possession whenever possible.

After another short drink break, Rodgers split his squad into three sections – defence, midfield and attack – for game-specific 10-minute drills. Kennedy took the defenders to work on defending crosses and basic high balls, focusing on shape and the preferred distance between the individual members of the back four in these circumstances.

Rodgers himself worked with three midfielders at a time. The players were set up in his favoured shape of one deep-lying controller and two advanced midfielders. Poles were used as markers and the drills focused on the distance between players, the fluidity of movement and ways in which to move off markers to create space to serve and receive passes in a tight midfield area.

Davies worked with attacking players on shooting drills into one of the main goals. Mannequins were used as defenders and Celtic's forwards focused on movement and passing combinations, before firing in shots from around the box.

After this section was complete, the players went back into their teams for another 15-minute game. This time, full-size goals were used in an area half-a-pitch long and 18 yards wide. There was no limit on touches but shape, movement and awareness were again the focus in a high-tempo contest. Rodgers stepped in on occasion to make some points, but the information was put across quickly.

With the game over, the session started to wind down. Two one-touch rondos, the piggy-in-the-middle passing exercises loved by Pep Guardiola, were set up for defenders and midfielders, while forwards including Sinclair and Leigh Griffiths worked on their penalty technique. After five minutes, the squad gathered together to stretch off for one last time before the session was brought to a close.

Yet for Celtic's sports science staff, the work didn't end there. Players wear GPS chips and heart monitors in every session, and their performances levels are monitored during the workouts. A computer at the side of the pitch produces live data and allows Driscoll and his staff to study the rate of perceived exertion (RPE) during sessions.

This gives an insight into how hard players are working and how much the session is taking out of them physically. It offers a valuable idea of an individual's level of conditioning and can also influence decisions on the intensity of training. All this data is also collated and analysed after every session, with reports produced for Rodgers.

The Celtic manager also has the training footage at

his disposal. Camera gantries are situated at the side of every training pitch at Lennoxtown and all sessions are filmed. This allows Rodgers and his staff to review the work from that day and analyse any areas of interest.

Nutrition is another important part of the post-training regime. The Celtic players have protein shakes and bars available from the moment they walk off the pitch and are encouraged to eat lunch and take on liquids as soon as possible after the session finishes, to begin the refuelling process.

Even in times of celebration, recovery is of paramount importance. In the Tynecastle away dressing room after Celtic clinched the title, a bottle of champagne was plonked on the leather treatment table as the players began their 'Championees' chant. Beside the bubbly were energy drinks, protein shakes and bottles of cherry juice. Celtic players are often seen clutching this dark liquid after games as it helps muscle recovery and aids sleep, due to its natural melatonin content.

Rob Naughton is Celtic's first-team nutritionist and spends one day per week at Lennoxtown, meeting with the players and staff. He produces plans, and remains in contact with them by telephone. He even encourages players to send him photographs of their meals via WhatsApp, for feedback and advice.

Rodgers and his staff will also have lunch at Lennoxtown but that has to fit around a hectic schedule of afternoon activity for the Celtic backroom team. For the manager, there are numerous daily meetings with players, where he communicates openly and offers feedback and support. The phone never stops ringing either, with Rodgers in daily contact with chief executive Peter Lawwell.

Opposition analysis is a key area for Rodgers and he spends hours looking at footage to prepare for forthcoming matches. Potential signings are also never far from his thinking and the Celtic manager will review clips of recommended targets as he and Lee Congerton, the club's head of recruitment, formulate transfer plans. Rodgers also spends a lot of time with Celtic's academy staff.

There are other club commitments too. From charity events to corporate obligations, the Celtic manager is rarely off duty. On media days, Rodgers could also have up to 90 minutes with the broadcasters, and the daily and Sunday newspapers. There are also contractual one-to-one interviews with the various TV rights-holders.

The Celtic manager does share the workload. Davies and Kennedy will speak individually to players and offer feedback, while also focusing on opposition analysis among various other duties. Goalkeeping coach Stevie Woods and Craig Gordon regularly review performance footage, study opposition players and look at trends in modern goalkeeping.

Overall, huge daily demands are placed on every single member of staff at Lennoxtown, from office workers to chefs, from security guards to those responsible for the upkeep of the training pitches. Rodgers expects total commitment from everyone but his own work ethic sets the tone.

"Our leader is someone who demands a certain level from himself," said Celtic assistant Davies. "He demands that level from the players and the staff. He expects you to meet that. Therefore, you become relentless. He can only demand that if he's demanded it from himself.

"I've seen managers who have made similar demands

of the players, without making those same demands of themselves. As a leader, Brendan's always been extremely hard-working, dedicated to his profession and a winner. Everyone feeds off that."

SCOTT BROWN

THE CELTIC WARRIOR

"I couldn't put a valuation on Scott Brown.
He is priceless for me."
Brendan Rodgers, May 3, 2017

THE constant pain in Scott Brown's hamstrings was compounded by the nagging doubt in his mind. Celtic's captain had just won his sixth Scottish league winners' medal in nine years at the club and should have been savouring every second of the title celebrations.

Yet after holding aloft the Premiership trophy on May 15, 2016, and leading Celtic on a lap of honour, Brown took a quiet moment to contemplate the future. Deep down, he wondered if this was the beginning of the end for him at the club.

Ronny Deila was on his way out as manager and Brown knew there were no guarantees that his successor would want him to remain as part of the squad, let alone as captain. The midfielder had been hampered by tendinitis in both hamstrings and various other niggles in the 2015/16 season. His form and influence had suffered as a result.

In the extra-time Scottish Cup semi-final defeat to Rangers on April 17, 2016, Brown completed 120 minutes but was clearly inhibited. He missed a penalty in the shoot-out but even the walk from the halfway line was a struggle. "I couldn't really twist and turn," he admitted months later. "It was sore getting out of bed and even sitting in the car. I felt aches and pains all the time."

On May 1, 2016, when Celtic effectively clinched a fifth successive championship by beating Hearts 3-1 at Tynecastle, Brown called it quits for the season and also pulled out of Scotland's summer friendlies against Italy and France. His body could take no more punishment. He underwent platelet-rich plasma treatment for his hamstring problems and didn't train for six weeks.

Brown hoped a summer of rest and recuperation would aid his recovery but still had to deal with reports of his demise across Scottish football. "Everyone was telling me I was finished," he said. Brown was on the verge of turning 31 and there were widespread whispers that his days as a dynamic driving force for Celtic were over. Even Brown himself had doubts over his future.

"I thought at the end of the 2015/16 season that my time at Celtic was slowly fading away," he said. "I had fallen out of love with football. I needed six weeks off to recharge the batteries and I thought, 'I'm going to give it one final push and do everything I can.'"

Brown also sought guidance from Scotland manager Gordon Strachan, the man who brought him to Celtic in

2007. The message was to ignore the doubters. "When you're 29 and you have a bad a game, you're shite," Strachan told him. "When you're 30 and have a bad game, your legs have gone." Brown took that advice on board. "I thought, 'Wee Stracho is right…I'm going out there to prove everyone wrong.'"

Then came the call from Brendan Rodgers. Brown was starting a break in London when the new Celtic manager was appointed on May 20. Within days, they had spoken on the phone. The new manager was instantly positive and keen to arrange a face-to-face meeting as soon as possible.

With Brown already in England, Rodgers invited the Celtic captain to his family home in London. They had dinner there and discussed football for four hours. Rodgers laid out his plans for Celtic and assured Brown that he wanted him to remain as captain and lead his revolution on the pitch.

The duo talked over their respective careers and discussed philosophies and tactics. Rodgers sought Brown's opinion on the strengths and weaknesses of the Celtic team he was inheriting and how he viewed his own position within the club, as captain and longest-serving player.

Strachan signed Brown from Hibernian in 2007 for £4.4million and Rodgers revealed that he had admired the midfielder from those early days as a swashbuckling, box-to-box tyro at Easter Road. The Celtic captain's game had evolved over the years but Rodgers felt he could still be a major influence as "the controller" of his team.

The Celtic manager's vision included Brown as a commanding, dominant midfield presence, regardless of formation. Rodgers believed he could dictate a high-tempo style, but reinforced the need for his captain to conserve his energy on the park and also look after his body off it. Brown's infamous night out early in the week of the 2015 League Cup final, when he was pictured slumped on a pavement, had gained attention across Britain at that time.

"I didn't know what Scott was like before," said Rodgers. "I'd only seen him from afar and had heard one or two things about his game from others. But I always judge for myself. My first impressions of him were very positive.

"When we met, I talked about lifestyle and looking after your body. I told him I wanted him to live and breathe football 24 hours a day and that he still has his best years ahead of him. I said to him, 'Minimum, if you look after your body, then you can go on until you are 35'.

"Scott readjusted his diet and took on board all the things we were trying to impose in terms of preparation, so we could complete this season at a really high level. He has adapted his lifestyle and you see it in the games. I look at his body and his physical shape, and he is in great condition. He is fit and strong.

"I've been fortunate to work with really good captains. I embrace them, let them know exactly how I work and they take their lead from that. With Scott, it was a case of looking at football in a different way, life in a different way and can you make yourself the best you can be?"

Refreshed by an extended break and invigorated by the trust placed in him by Rodgers, Brown returned for pre-season with renewed vigour. Within a couple of weeks, word spread that the Celtic captain was flying.

His first pre-season start, against Olimpija Ljubljana, reinforced that view. Brown's sharpness had returned. He already appeared transformed by the new regime.

Yet even the Celtic captain wouldn't have envisaged just how influential he would be in his first season under Rodgers, clocking up 54 games in all competitions. He developed a close relationship with Rodgers and only dropped out of the team due to suspension or being rested. "Scott is a remarkable leader, a real warrior," said the Celtic manager.

It was his tenth season at Celtic but Brown had never looked fitter or played with more composure. His rejuvenation under Rodgers was incredible. "The gaffer backed me 100 per cent," said Brown. "He's always been there for me and he believed in me."

The strength of Brown's relationship with Rodgers could be seen in the handling of his Scotland conundrum. The Celtic captain retired from international duty in August in order to get extra rest and protect his fitness, but his club form led to him and Scotland manager Strachan discussing the possibility of a rethink in time for a World Cup qualifier against England in November.

It was a delicate situation but they handled it with maturity. Rodgers had reservations but understood Brown's loyalty to Strachan, the man who brought him to Celtic. He was also sympathetic to the Scotland manager's situation. Brown was in the form of his life and Strachan needed his top-level experience and influence for Wembley and beyond.

Proof of the midfielder's elevated performance levels could be taken from his Champions League statistics. In six group matches against Barcelona, Borussia

Monchengladbach and Manchester City, Brown ran an average of 11.78km per game and had a pass completion rate of 95 per cent. Out of his 411 attempted passes, 393 were successful. Of the players who had featured in six group games, only PSG defender Marquinos had better passing stats. In the 3-3 draw with City at Celtic Park, Brown produced arguably his best performance of the season against Pep Guardiola's world-class team.

"Scott was playing against some of the top midfield players in the world in one of the top teams in Europe and he dominated the midfield," said Rodgers. "He is highly-gifted technically. He has a wonderful touch, wonderful awareness of where he is in the field, he can play short, he can play long.

"The biggest compliment I can give Scott is, if I look at my Liverpool team that nearly won the title, he would definitely have been in it. But thankfully Scott's chosen to play nearly 10 years at Celtic. He could have played in England but he was happy in his life at Celtic."

Brown's Champions League performances proved there is more to him than the popular image of the glaring midfield enforcer. He is self-deprecating in interviews and rarely misses a chance to play down his own talents with a joke. At 31, he is still a hyperactive member of the Celtic team, constantly laughing and listening to the same booming techno music he did as a teenager.

Yet Rodgers knew an intelligent footballer when he saw one. Whether it was a 3-4-3 or 4-2-3-1 formation, Brown understood what his manager wanted and ensured Celtic stuck to their shape and implemented the game-plan. "Tactically Scott does everything I want him to do, and that tells me he thinks clearly under pressure," said the Celtic manager. Rodgers' intense training enthused Brown. He had criticised Deila's sessions as "slow" and "not hard enough", but he relished life under the new manager. Celtic's fitness staff were often heard urging Brown to slow down as he led from the front on the Lennoxtown training pitches. "I now have a smile on my face coming in every morning," he said.

On rare occasions, Brown was deployed as one of two advanced midfielders in Rodgers' 4-3-3 formation, yet he was mostly used deeper. This allowed him to drop back in between Celtic's central defenders and get on the ball. Brown's job was to make angular forward passes to get the team up the pitch and ensure Celtic won the physical battle.

Brown played on the edge at all times. He accumulated 16 bookings in all competitions but only once took it too far and saw red. His lunge on Liam Boyce in the 2-2 draw with Ross County on April 16 came during an explosive end to the Premiership game in Dingwall, which saw referee Don Robertson conned by Alex Schalk's dive for a controversial penalty.

Brown would have missed the Scottish Cup semi-final against Rangers due to an automatic two-game suspension, but Celtic had the right to appeal and the SFA hearing was postponed for a week due to an Easter Bank Holiday. It was viewed as a stroke of good fortune for the player and club, but Celtic ultimately won the appeal as the red card was reduced to a yellow.

Brown's availability for that Hampden semi-final was a relief for Rodgers. He won the man-of-the-match award as he strolled through the 2-0 win, running it from start to finish. This didn't surprise the Celtic manager. In the most important domestic games, his captain had been dominant. He bossed Joey Barton and the rest of the Rangers midfield in the 5-1 Celtic Park victory in September. On New Year's Eve at Ibrox, he dragged Rodgers' team to a higher level of performance after a sluggish start. His late tackle on James Tavernier in 23 minutes earned him a booking but was clearly designed to wake Celtic up. Brown didn't even look at the referee waving the card. He simply turned and started shouting at his team-mates. He demanded more from every Celtic player and he got it. Brown played a true captain's role in the 2-1 win.

In the Betfred Cup final against Aberdeen, he was similarly influential in a surprisingly comfortable 3-0 victory. Brown set the tone for Celtic with his pressing, passing and on-pitch organisation. He offered defensive protection to allow Tom Rogic to excel in an advanced position and one casual backheel pass in a congested midfield summed up Brown's accomplished performance.

"It's a great honour to win a trophy for Celtic with Scott as my captain," said Rodgers. "He was outstanding in the way he controlled the game and dominated the midfield. He pulls the team together on the pitch."

Rodgers realised early on that Celtic were a more effective team with Brown's presence. The other players looked up to him and responded to the regular verbal volleys he fired in their direction. In almost a decade at the club, he had won everything in Scotland and operated at the highest level in the Champions League.

"The players take a great lead from him," said the Celtic manager. "He's at the very front from the first steps we take onto the training field, the warm-up, right from the very start. He's up for every game and never has a lazy day. He is very similar to Steven Gerrard. Scott's ambition is for the club, not for himself. That's what you find in these types of players. They are not selfish. Everything they do is based around what's best for the team and they put themselves secondary to that.

"Steven, like Scott, was a wonderful ambassador for his club. In the changing room they are very strong, they are able to lead. You need your lieutenants in there who can control that and certainly Scott is one of them."

Even on the rare occasions Brown was having a poor match, Rodgers knew his captain would never hide. If the midfielder misplaced a pass, he would still make himself available again when Celtic won possession back. Brown was comfortable with the responsibility placed on his shoulders.

"Scott had an absolute beast," said Rodgers, after Brown's unusually poor performance in Celtic's 5-0 title-clinching win over Hearts. "But I would never take him off. That's the jungle in that midfield area, and there's no better man to have in the jungle than Scott Brown. Even when he is having a shocker."

Rodgers labelled Brown as "the most influential player in Scottish football" and expressed his shock that his captain didn't make the PFA Scotland Player of the Year shortlist. "You talk about influence and you judge in the big pressure games," said Rodgers. "How many times have you seen the influence of Scott Brown? His level has been unbelievable throughout the season."

Yet, despite the lack of individual recognition by his fellow professionals, by the end of the season Brown had taken his Celtic trophy haul to 13, with 11 as captain. Only Billy McNeill has led the club to more silverware. He also replaced the legendary Lisbon Lions captain at the top of Celtic's European appearance list, lifting his tally to 77. That helped him break through the 400-mark for overall Celtic appearances and cemented his status as a club great.

THE PURSUIT OF HAPPINESS

This is how it feels to be Celtic,
Champions again as you know.
Brendan Rodgers is here for 10 in a row
10 in a row

BRENDAN RODGERS weighed up the question and broke into a wide smile. "I was just stretching my fingers," said the Celtic manager, when asked if he had made a 10-in-a-row gesture after the 3-1 win over Kilmarnock on April 8, 2017. Some 20 minutes earlier, he had raised both hands to the air on the pitch as the Celtic fans serenaded him with his own chant, to the tune of Inspiral Carpets' *This Is How It Feels*.

This became a favourite among the Celtic support around the time a sixth successive Premiership title was secured against Hearts a week earlier. Most initially sang in hope, rather than expectation. The dominant narrative around the Scottish game during that period was that four more years of Rodgers at Celtic was highly unlikely. Given the standard of his work, English offers were inevitable.

Then came an email from Celtic's public relations department at 11.55am on Friday, April 7. It was short and to the point. The weekly media conference had been moved from Lennoxtown to Celtic Park for a major announcement. By 2.30pm, Rodgers was sitting next to chief executive Peter Lawwell inside the No.7 restaurant after signing a new four-year contract. The 6 + 4 calculation was instant. Maybe that new song wasn't wishful thinking from the fans after all.

Sealing a deal to bring Rodgers to the club in May 2016 was a major coup for Celtic. But convincing him to commit for another four years seemed too good to be true. Premier League club owners, many of whom saw Rodgers as a potential future manager, must have raised an eyebrow. Yet his reason for accepting the new Celtic contract was simple: You can't put a price on happiness.

"There is not a place I could be in this world right now where I'd be happier in my football life and personal life," said Rodgers. "Happiness is the key. If you're not happy then it doesn't matter how much money you get, you can't work very well. I drive into Celtic Park and it's like driving into the best cathedral in the world.

"There are maybe possibilities to have gone to the Premier League. That is how it works if you are doing well, you get linked. But I would forfeit all that to be here and happy. This is a club I love and know well. I could be a manager until I'm 60, so that gives me another 16 years, but in these next four years I want to give everything to Celtic. Of course there might be challenges down the line but I don't think I'll ever get bored of managing Celtic. "I've had five jobs in my career so far, so I'm thinking at some point I need to just stay calm. I've already worked in the English Premier League and I cannot think of a better place for me to be at this stage of my life than Glasgow Celtic. I'm very comfortable here and sometimes, that ambition, you have to be careful. You have to really appreciate what you have.

"I was very honoured when the club came to me. Four years might be a term that would frighten other managers. But for me it just felt so right. I feel really at home here. I still feel there's a lot of work I want to give. We've only started. The journey has only just begun and there's a lot of differences that I still feel I can make.

"I have a special feeling here. I am a Celtic fan myself so I know exactly what the people think and what they want, from the board to the guy sat in his seat watching the game. I want to try and bring them as far to that as I possibly can. When my time is up, hopefully I will have left a legacy here that they can smile about and have enjoyed. Then it'll be over to the next one."

Offering a four-year contract to a manager was a major departure for Celtic. Like Martin O'Neill, Gordon Strachan, Neil Lennon and Ronny Deila, Rodgers had initially operated on a rolling one-year deal. This had been Celtic's preferred way of working for over a decade. It suited both the club and manager. If Celtic wanted to terminate the contract, they paid up 12 months of wages. If the manager was lured elsewhere, the club's compensation was fixed at the same level.

But Rodgers had lived up to the "special" billing given to him by Lawwell at his unveiling in May 2016. Just 11 months later, Celtic's chief executive had seen enough to state that his club had a "world-class" operator at the helm. Those words were backed up by finance. Celtic were willing to offer a new four-year contract worth over £10million to keep Rodgers at the club.

The full terms weren't disclosed but the new, long-term agreement appeared to offer Celtic extra financial protection should another club make a play for their manager. Yet the board was keen to stress that this wasn't just a cynical ploy to maximise compensation. Instead, it was a massive show of faith in Rodgers, a reward for his success and transformational impact at the club, and a statement of intent for the future.

"An insurance policy wasn't the motivation," said Lawwell. "Our judgment is a four-year contract is worth it. The message it sends out is that he is staying with Celtic. Don't bother, don't waste your time. The message is clear. We want him here for at least the length of his contract. We have plans. We have ambition. There is an expectation from the supporters and he is fundamental to it.

"At Celtic, we'll be flexible with debt but we'll never put the club in jeopardy and Brendan gets that. If you believe in that, you can't have money to buy the best, you have to create the best and that's what he is; a creator and developer. We want the same things, we work well, we understand each other and he's a delight to work with.

"I do believe he's a world-class manager. I've been here for 14 years now and worked with five different managers. They're all great managers but I definitely think Brendan is world class. He would be nearer the full package. Technically, tactically he is exceptional.

"He's surpassed all our expectations but the most surprising thing is that he's done it with the same squad.

That shows one of his main strengths is making players better. He has come in and taken them to another level. That's what we need, creating, developing, building teams as opposed to buying them. He's demonstrated his excellence in doing that."

Rodgers also felt a sense of duty to his Celtic players. He had convinced Moussa Dembele and Scott Sinclair to sign for the club the previous summer, while Craig Gordon, Tom Rogic, Kieran Tierney, Mikael Lustig and James Forrest had all agreed new long-term contracts. Rodgers wanted to make it clear that he planned to be there with them.

"It was going to be very hard for me to sit with all these boys and ask them to commit their futures to Celtic with me on a one-year rolling contract," said Rodgers. "Players will always look at the manager and see how long he is connected to the club. If I am committed to the club fully, that makes it a little bit easier for them to make that decision. That is important."

Rodgers has a long-term vision for taking the club forward. Parts of Lennoxtown resembled a building site towards the end of his first season as a seven-figure refurbishment on the training ground facilities kicked in. There were longer term plans put in place to create a new state-of-the-art indoor training area, in time for the winter months.

At Celtic Park, a new Desso hybrid pitch was being installed to ensure the best possible quality of playing surface. Lee Congerton, at Rodgers' behest, had been appointed to take control of Celtic's recruitment and help improve the squad.

In a domestic sense, Celtic were untouchable. Yet Rodgers wanted to succeed with even more style than he did in his maiden season. In European competition, there were even more objectives to target. Could Celtic get to the Champions League group stages again? Could they reach the knockout rounds, or gain parachute entry into the Europa League last 32? This drove Rodgers on.

"As a coach, I couldn't ask for a bigger challenge, to make Celtic a force in Europe without the finances available at other clubs," he said. "That's why I signed for four years. We want to dominate Scottish football, get into the Champions League and look to make a mark in Europe. The way we are building, that's the length of time I see will help us do that.

"If I went back to the Premier League I'd have gone into millions upon millions of pounds, where it's all about buying. What is forgotten about is nurturing players. We're a blue-chip club who will always want top players. But we also have to bring young ones through and that's the challenge I'm looking forward to. Can we continue with this run while growing and developing a team for the Champions League?

"I want to develop young players and bring in experienced ones who can be good influences. Also I have to find a way of playing that's synonymous with Celtic. Just like what I had with Swansea. We didn't have the best individuals there. But we had a collective that was really strong and that allowed us to beat the best teams. That's what we have to do here when we're on that stage."

Rodgers constantly referred to "we" and "us" when talking about his new contract and plans for the future. On the pitch, his Celtic team was very much about the collective, but that extended to his backroom staff. This was shown when Rodgers, upon receiving his October

Manager of the Month award, insisted that six members of his team were present for the official photograph.

Assistant manager Chris Davies, first-team coach John Kennedy, goalkeeping coach Stevie Woods, head of performance Glen Driscoll, head of sports science Jack Nayler and sports scientist John Currie all joined him to receive the award. After signing his new contract, Rodgers pointed to Davies and Driscoll's fulfilling Celtic experience as being proof that contentment in a job is priceless.

"Most people in football know the size of Celtic but you never truly know the scale of it," said Rodgers. "The two boys who joined me had been around the game for a while. I was trying to explain to them why it was the move for us. There was more financial gains to go elsewhere but I told them it would be great for us.

"You speak to them now, nine months on, and they just have sighs of happiness every day at Lennoxtown. It's unbelievable. You can't buy that. I've been on the big wages in England before and I know it will come again, another time. But it's about being happy."

TINSELTOWN IN THE RAIN

S IR ALEX FERGUSON pauses for a second as 20,000 people inside the SSE Hydro hang on his every word. The legendary Scottish manager is in Glasgow to pay tribute to the Lisbon Lions at Celtic's 'Celebrate '67' extravaganza. Gazing out at the crowd from a lectern, Ferguson says: "If you gave a Hollywood director this story of Jock Stein and Celtic, they would claim it was fiction."

That European Cup win on May 25, 1967 will always be the No.1 Celtic blockbuster, but producing sequels has never been a problem for the club. Two days after Ferguson's stirring tribute to the Lions, Brendan Rodgers' class of 2017 summoned up a spectacular, dramatic finale to their Treble-winning Invincible season that would also be deemed too good to be true in Tinseltown.

"Magical" was how Tom Rogic described Celtic's 2-1 Scottish Cup final win over Aberdeen. The Hampden earth had moved for the Australian 13 months earlier when the ball bobbled just before he skied his penalty over the bar to condemn Celtic to a semi-final defeat against Rangers in the same competition. This time, a bolt of lightning struck the rain-soaked national stadium as Rogic waltzed into the box to score an injury-time winner and gain redemption. "Maybe it was all meant to be," he said.

But the fairytale didn't end there. Rodgers, a boyhood Celtic fan, had masterminded the Invincible Treble. No other team in Scottish football history had completed a domestic clean sweep without losing a game. Rodgers, in his first season, also became only the third Celtic manager to win the Treble, joining Stein and Martin O'Neill. "It feels surreal and it's an honour," he said. "Maybe the stars were aligned this year."

Then there was Kieran Tierney's emotional sub-plot, which tugged at the heartstrings of even the most hardened supporter. Mr Celtic, as team-mate Patrick Roberts christened him, was left with shattered teeth and a damaged jaw after being caught by Aberdeen's Jayden Stockley in the first half. Tierney's final was over as he was rushed to the Scottish Centre for Excellence in Dentistry in Govan for emergency treatment from Celtic's dentist, Arshad Ali.

Yet nothing would stop him from returning for the celebrations. He arrived back at the stadium car park just as Celtic captain Scott Brown was leading the team up the Hampden steps. But with Aberdeen fans departing in their thousands, the vehicle was unable to get in. Tierney refused to wait. Still dressed in his Celtic kit and boots, he jumped out and sprinted through a sea of red shirts towards the Hampden front door.

Tierney got there just in time and claimed one of the biggest cheers of the afternoon from the Celtic support when he appeared. It was fitting that the lifelong fan was the last player to show off the Scottish Cup on such a historic occasion. The teenager punched the Celtic badge on his chest in an outpouring of raw emotion. He was in pain but nothing would stop him savouring that moment. Like the rest of his Celtic team-mates, he was an Invincible Treble-winner.

That's what Rodgers had urged his players to become when he gathered them together inside the Hampden home dressing room for their pre-match address, around 10 minutes before kick-off. He evoked the spirit of Lisbon in his team-talk, 50 years and two days on from that triumph. But he also warned his players they couldn't rely on fate. They had to take control of their own destiny.

"I said to them that this is a final that you want people to write about afterwards," said Rodgers. "But you have to make history – it doesn't just happen. The players showed remarkable courage to get the result and create their own history. To go 47 domestic games unbeaten and win three trophies is an incredible achievement. It's monumental."

Celtic's run to the Scottish Cup final began with routine wins against Albion Rovers and Inverness Caledonian Thistle. Nine goals were scored and none were conceded as Rodgers' side set up a home quarter-final against St Mirren. Then struggling at the bottom of the Championship, Jack Ross' well-drilled team led at half-time before a second-half goal blitz ensured a 4-1 victory for Celtic.

Up next were Rangers on April 23 as Celtic were

handed a chance to finally avenge the semi-final defeat of 12 months earlier. Rodgers had been in Belfast that day, at his nephew Malachy's christening, but remembered the shock from his family members as news of Celtic's defeat on penalties came through.

"I was surrounded by lots of people in the chapel on their phones," he recalled. "I was always up to speed with the score. Then I watched the game later. Celtic could still have won it despite not playing so well. But Rangers were the better team and deserved to go through."

A year had passed since that Hampden meeting but it felt like a lifetime. Both clubs had changed managers, Rodgers replacing Ronny Deila and Pedro Caixinha coming in for Mark Warburton at Ibrox. The Portuguese coach inherited a squad lacking genuine quality and bereft of confidence when he took over in March. Celtic, in stark contrast, were thriving under Rodgers.

There were nine survivors from that shoot-out defeat by Rangers but the dominant performances of Mikael Lustig, Dedryck Boyata and Brown in a comfortable 2-0 win were symbolic of a team completely transformed under the new manager. "We know if we turned up we are the best in Scotland," said Brown. "They don't have the legs or the quality we have."

Caixinha later revealed he'd instructed his players to leave Lustig on the ball at right-back and shut off the space down Celtic's left wing. That plan backfired spectacularly when the Swede's raking pass found Moussa Dembele, who fed Callum McGregor for a casual finish. Scott Sinclair's second-half penalty then killed off the game.

"I saw everything I would want from the team in terms of composure, temperament and tactical quality," said Rodgers. "We were absolutely brilliant and 12 months on from where the team was last year, it really shows the level they have gone to."

With the Premiership title and Betfred Cup already secured, Celtic were now under pressure to add the Scottish Cup to their collection and complete a rare Treble, only the fourth in the club's history. "Everybody was hyping it up for months, to the extent that it's almost the case that if we hadn't done it, a lot of people outside the club would have been happy about that," said McGregor.

The Invincibles tag added another layer of expectancy. Celtic's historic unbeaten Premiership record was secured six days before the Scottish Cup final. Perhaps unfairly, defeat at Hampden against Aberdeen would have taken a shine off that achievement and Rodgers sensed all was not right within his squad two days before the final.

"We've had one bad training session since I've been here and that was on Thursday before playing Aberdeen," said Rodgers. "I cut it short. I walked inside. The quality wasn't good enough of what we demand. Maybe there was something floating around in their minds about how we had won the league. Maybe there was a wee celebratory feel, but the session was stopped."

Rodgers made his displeasure clear to his players. It was the second last session of the season but he simply wouldn't tolerate levels dropping. "That's not how we work," he said. "We set a standard right at the beginning." It was the jolt the Celtic players needed. The Friday session, held 24 hours before the final, was conducted exactly how the manager wanted.

By that afternoon, Rodgers had settled on his starting

line-up for Hampden. There were no surprises. Dembele was only fit enough to take a place on the bench, so Leigh Griffiths started at the focal point of Celtic's attack.

The Scotland striker had endured a frustrating campaign. A prolific opening spell under Rodgers was halted when he was injured in early September. Dembele claimed the jersey and Griffiths struggled to win it back. A string of niggling injuries didn't help his case but Rodgers also felt his basic conditioning needed to improve as he delivered a public rebuke in January. "Talent is not enough," he said.

The Celtic manager warned Griffiths that he had to work harder every day in training and completely devote his life to football. Rodgers told him he had to be ready to cope with the demands of playing in his high-pressing, aggressive style. Griffiths took that advice on board and knuckled down. When Dembele pulled up against Rangers in the Scottish Cup semi-final, he grabbed his chance.

Griffiths won the penalty that sealed Celtic's place in the final and then claimed four goals and five assists in the five post-split fixtures in the league. There was also a tantrum after being subbed during Celtic's 5-0 win over Partick Thistle. Rodgers gave Griffiths a death stare after his strop, before planting a kiss on his cheek at full-time. The Celtic striker later apologised as Rodgers assured him his cup final involvement would not be hampered by his fit of pique.

Roberts also emerged as a key player in the final two months of the season, ousting James Forrest from the right side of Celtic's attack. On loan from Manchester City, he blossomed under Rodgers' guidance and rejected the chance to play for England at the FIFA U-20

World Cup in South Korea to stay for Celtic's Treble bid. "The chance to make history at this club is important to me," said Roberts.

By the time the team bus pulled into Hampden's underground tunnel, Celtic were ready, but Rodgers had a surprise in store. The previous night, during a team meeting, he had used a projector to display individual messages of support for every player from their families. When they entered the dressing room to prepare for the game the next day, those same messages had been placed inside envelopes and sat next to the players' lockers.

It took a lot of planning, but that touch meant a lot to Rodgers' players. Lustig later posted an Instagram photograph of his message from wife Josefin and daughters Lucia and Lexie: 'Mikael, Beach ball, derby goal, rabona – can't wait to see what happens next season. Love you.'

Celtic were mentally and physically prepared, but Aberdeen tested their resolve with Jonny Hayes' early opener. Questions were being asked as Rodgers' players restarted the game but the response was instant. Celtic kept the ball and worked an opening for Stuart Armstrong to bury a left-foot shot past Joe Lewis for the equaliser.

Rodgers let his players dry off at half-time before reiterating the need to stay calm. Aberdeen were operating a man-marking system in certain areas and the Celtic manager was convinced they would tire eventually. He urged his players to shift the ball quickly, to move their opponents around the pitch and just wait for their legs to go. "Space will open up," he told them, and he was right.

Celtic survived a scare early in the second half when

Jonny Hayes' square ball fell behind Kenny McLean at the end of a promising breakaway. It was a pivotal moment as Celtic then stepped through the gears against tiring opponents. The mental and physical fitness Rodgers had spoken about so often in Slovenia during pre-season came to the fore. It was death by football for Aberdeen. As the game drew to a close, they were running out of lives as Celtic spurned a series of chances.

The heavens had opened over Hampden. Right on cue, there was a bolt of lightning and clap of thunder just as Rogic entered the Aberdeen box. The clock showed 91 minutes but time stood still as the Australian jinked past Andrew Considine and beat Lewis from the tightest of angles.

Rodgers raised his hands to the sky as Rogic ran straight into the arms of the elated Celtic supporters down by the corner flag. This was history. Celtic had secured an Invincible Treble.

"It's probably the best feeling you can have on a football pitch to score the winner in the last minute and then jump into the crowd," said Rogic. "It was an amazingly proud moment for me. It's a perfect end to a special season. To go unbeaten domestically, to get the Treble, it's just amazing. It's something that we will look back on forever."

Roberts, who embraced his close friend Tierney at the end, continued in a similar theme. "When I look back on my career, this will be the biggest highlight, my biggest accomplishment in the game."

Lustig choked back tears on the pitch as he tried to express his emotions. "It feels amazing, we can all retire now," he smiled.

McGregor, who had been at the club since primary school, gave a revealing insight into the Celtic players' awareness of how much expectancy was on their shoulders, just days after the Lisbon Lions' 50th anniversary. "It's been an emotional week and it was in our minds that we had to give the fans another great moment," he said.

"The Lisbon Lions stuff was inspirational for us. You're writing yourself into the history of Celtic Football Club. You know how big and important that history is, so what we've managed to do is really special."

For Celtic captain Brown, it was the dream end to his tenth season at the club. He raised three fingers at the end to symbolise his first Treble at the club, infuriating the Aberdeen fans he was standing in front of, but could have been forgiven for raising another two to all those who had written him off at the end of the previous campaign.

"It's the best feeling I've ever had in football," said Brown. "The fact the final went down to the last minute sums us up. For the 10 years I've been at Celtic this is the best, most determined bunch of lads I've ever played with. This is the biggest achievement anyone could ask for.

"When you go back to that first game in Gibraltar, I don't think anyone would have expected this. For us to go all the way through the season undefeated and to win three trophies, that's phenomenal, just phenomenal."

Rodgers embraced every single player and member of staff on the Hampden pitch and then shared a moment inside the dressing room with Dermot Desmond, Peter Lawwell and Celtic's board members. They congratulated and thanked him for his work in transforming the team.

Rodgers' reply was simple. Leading Celtic through such a special season had been an honour. "I was born into Celtic and it's a huge privilege to manage this club," said Rodgers. "It's been a dream. I couldn't have written the script for this season any better."

Invincible

CREDITS

Invincible
Brendan Rodgers was speaking to the Scottish daily and Sunday newspapers, and BT Sport. Callum McGregor and Mikael Lustig were speaking to the Scottish daily newspapers.

One Vision, One Club
Brendan Rodgers was speaking to the Scottish daily and Sunday newspapers, and Sky Sports.

More than a Job
Brendan Rodgers was speaking to the Scottish daily and Sunday newspaper, and Celtic TV. Kieran McMullan was speaking to the Scottish daily newspapers. Ronny Deila was speaking to the author. Chris Davies was speaking to the Scottish daily newspapers. Mikael Lustig was speaking to Expressen.

Los Detallitos
Brendan Rodgers was speaking to the Scottish daily and Sunday newspapers. John Kennedy was speaking to the Scottish daily newspapers.

Shock and Awe
Brendan Rodgers and Roy Chipolina were speaking to the Scottish daily newspapers.

Never Die Wondering
Brendan Rodgers was speaking to the Scottish daily and Sunday newspapers. Leigh Griffiths was speaking to BT Sport. Roy Keane was speaking on ITV Sport.

Local Knowledge
Brendan Rodgers and Jack Ross were speaking to
Scottish daily newspapers.

Scott Sinclair: The Logical One
Scott Sinclair was speaking to The Times, The Daily Mail
and Scottish daily newspapers. Brendan Rodgers was
speaking to the Scottish daily newspapers.

He Ain't in my League
Joey Barton was speaking to talkSPORT. Leigh Griffiths
was speaking to the Scottish daily newspapers. Scott
Brown was speaking to Sky Sports and the Scottish
daily newspapers. Brendan Rodgers was speaking to the
Scottish Sunday newspapers.

A Nou Level
Brendan Rodgers was speaking to the Scottish daily
and Sunday newspapers. Neil Lennon was speaking to
Graham Hunter. Scott Brown and Erik Sviatchenko were
speaking to the Scottish daily newspapers.

Cum on Feel the Noize
Brendan Rodgers was speaking to the Scottish daily and
Sunday newspapers. Leigh Griffiths was speaking to the
Scottish daily newspapers.

Moussa Dembele: The Wolf of Kerrydale Street
Mamadi Fofana was speaking to the author. Moussa
Dembele and Brendan Rodgers were speaking to the
Scottish daily newspapers.

A Suitcase Full of Dreams
Brendan Rodgers and Patrick Roberts were speaking to the Scottish daily newspapers.

Adapt and Fly
Brendan Rodgers was speaking to the Scottish daily newspapers and the BBC. Stuart Armstrong was speaking to the official Celtic website.

Follow the Star
Brendan Rodgers was speaking to the Scottish daily and Sunday newspapers. Mikael Lustig was speaking to the Scottish daily newspapers.

Craig Gordon: Old Dog, New Tricks
Craig Gordon was speaking to the Scottish daily newspapers and Graham Hunter. Brendan Rodgers was speaking to the Scottish daily newspapers.

The Next Generation
Brendan Rodgers was speaking to the Scottish daily newspapers.

Kieran Tierney: From Ballboy to top Bhoy
Kieran Tierney was speaking to the Scottish daily and Sunday newspapers. Brendan Rodgers, Scott Sinclair and Ronny Deila were speaking to the Scottish daily newspapers.

Lennoxtown: A Day in the Life
Scott Brown was speaking to the Ladbrokes Football Show. Chris Davies was speaking to the Scottish Sunday newspapers.

Scott Brown: The Celtic Warrior
Scott Brown was speaking to the Ladbrokes Football
Show and the Scottish daily newspapers. Brendan
Rodgers was speaking to the Scottish daily newspapers.

The Pursuit of Happiness
Brendan Rodgers was speaking to the Scottish daily and
Sunday newspapers. Peter Lawwell was speaking to the
Scottish daily newspapers.

Tinseltown in the Rain
Brendan Rodgers was speaking to BBC Scotland and
the Scottish Sunday newspapers. Tom Rogic, Callum
McGregor, Patrick Roberts and Scott Brown were
speaking to the Scottish daily and Sunday newspapers.

In addition, the following sources helped with my
research for the book: Sky Sports' Goals on Sunday,
beIN Sports, talkSPORT, Official Celtic website, Celtic
TV, The Bleacher Report, Official Liverpool website, The
Anfield Wrap, This Is Anfield, The Ladbrokes Football
Show, The Daily Mail online, BBC Scotland, BT Sport,
Sky Sports, The Big Interview with Graham Hunter,
Michael Calvin's 'Life on the Volcano', TalkingBaws,
WalesOnline, The Guardian, The Independent.

ACKNOWLEDGEMENTS

THE battered old Spanish taxi was winding its way up the E15 motorway when my mobile phone rang. At the other end of the line was a BBC Radio Five Live producer, asking if I could come on the show to discuss Celtic's 1-0 defeat by Lincoln Red Imps in the Champions League qualifier. By then, the Shock of Gibraltar was headline news.

"How did that happen?" was the general gist of the conversation. Nursing a cold beer with the rest of the Scottish press pack an hour later, we were still trying to come up with an explanation. It was July 12, 2016, and day 16 of Brendan Rodgers' first Celtic trip, which had taken us from Slovenia to Spain and then Gibraltar. Nobody saw the defeat coming.

The Celtic manager remained calm. He felt it was simply a false start to his reign and he was right. But few could have predicted the events of the next 11 months as Celtic became Scotland's Invincibles and completed only the fourth domestic Treble in the club's history without losing a single game.

Rodgers' transformational impact on the team, individual players and club as a whole was incredible to witness. From Astana to Aberdeen, Monchengladbach to Motherwell, I covered around 40 Celtic games for the Scottish Sun newspaper. Watching this football revolution up close was fascinating.

It was a historic season. Champions League qualification kicked it all off but Celtic really excelled domestically. 47 matches, 43 wins, four draws, zero defeats and three trophies. An Invincible Treble is unprecedented in Scottish football but Celtic pulled it off, and did it in style, too. This is a unique story and one which deserves to be told. Not just for the here and now, but for the future. This Celtic team didn't scale the heights of the Lisbon Lions but 50 years on from that European Cup win, they couldn't have done any more to honour the memory of Jock Stein and his band of brothers.

My thanks firstly go to Brendan and all the Celtic players for their time during the course of the season. Brendan has always been open and engaging in hundreds of press conference interviews, while it's been a pleasure speaking to Scott Brown and his team-mates at locations across Scotland and Europe. Thanks also to Peter Lawwell, Iain Jamieson and Rhona Macdonald at Celtic.

Mamadi Fofana gave a gripping account of his client Moussa Dembele's pivotal first meeting with Brendan in London and was a huge help. My thanks go to him and Moussa, one of the most grounded young footballers you could hope to meet.

My friends at The Scottish Sun deserve a huge mention. Roger Hannah was supportive from the outset, while Robert Grieve and Derek McGregor were always keen to assist in any way they could. John Hartson remains a true gentleman of the game. Thanks for your help, big man.

Likewise, I'd like to thank my colleagues at other Scottish newspapers and media outlets for their probing questions and companionship as I pieced together the story of the season. Rivals during the day and allies at night, it's been a pleasure manning the mixed zones and sharing the transcriptions with all of you. Eating broccoli for breakfast in Kazakhstan remains a highlight.

A special mention to Hugh MacDonald for his priceless advice and guidance towards the end of the writing process. Thanks also to Kenny Ramsay, Scotland's top snapper, for the photos that capture the story of the season.

Above all, I want to give a huge thanks to Martin Greig and Neil White of BackPage, who were supportive of the book from our very first meeting. It's been a pleasure working with the guys and seeing their talent, vision and ambition at close quarters.

To Mum, Dad and the rest of the Friel clan, thanks for everything. Finally, my love and thanks to my wife Emma for her patience and understanding during all the late nights and early mornings spent tapping away at the laptop. It's finished now. Promise.

David Friel
May 29, 2017

ABOUT THE AUTHOR

David Friel has worked in journalism since 2004. A Strathclyde University graduate in History, he started off at the Kirkintilloch Herald. From there, he spent four years at the Celtic View between 2006 and 2010, covering the Gordon Strachan years and Celtic's two runs to the last 16 of the Champions League.

After a brief spell in the world of Scottish local government, David joined the Scottish Sun newspaper as a football writer in May 2012. Based in Glasgow, he covers all teams in Scotland but has reported extensively on Celtic's fortunes under Neil Lennon, Ronny Deila and Brendan Rodgers.

During the 2016/17 season, David covered the majority of Celtic's domestic and Champions League games, gaining a true insight into a historic Invincibles campaign.